CONCILIUM

Religion in the Seventies

CONCILIUM

Concilium, **November 1977: Spirituality**

CHARISMS IN THE CHURCH

Edited by
Christian Duquoc and
Casiano Floristan

A CROSSROAD BOOK
The Seabury Press • New York

1978
The Seabury Press
815 Second Avenue
New York, N.Y. 10017

Library of Congress Catalog Card Number: 78-53986
ISBN: 0-8164-0367-8
ISBN: 0-8164-2168-4 (pbk.)
Printed in the United States of America

CONTENTS

v

Part II
Bulletins

Editorial

THE last few years have seen the birth of a number of spontaneous movements, above all in the Catholic Church. They have brought a renewal of prayer and summoned people to evangelical action. They have emphasized the necessity of mysticism in a Church devoted to the word or to action. They have drawn attention to a long-obscure phenomenon: charisms.

To secular ears or to traditional Catholics the word 'charism' sounds rather odd, alien indeed, for it has no currency in ordinary modern English. This indifference to (or at best ignorance of) 'charisms' affects the very structure of the Catholic Church. A long history of opposition to heresies, to sectarian movements, to quasi-mystical phenomena and to messianic utopias has marked the present model of the Church. The institutionalized sacraments are preponderant in a form where the priestly or episcopal minister is the essential organizer. The ecclesial power is in the hands of those fully committed to the running of the institution; to such a degree, therefore, that they have given up any claim to raising a family and, until recently, also renounced the possibility of a trade or profession. This instrumental power does not, on the other hand, exclude but instead encourages recourse to the non-socializable practice of inwardness or the operation of grace.

The sacramental institution is thought to assist an unsurpassable personal link with God. Between the institution and that inward state, therefore, there is no middle term. The official ministers of the Church are suspicious of movements which are not the direct products of the institution. The charismatic movements, on the other hand, are not afraid of breaking with the unique sacramental instance and its support by a ministerial or priestly monopoly, and try to avoid any flight into an inwardness without social expression and any precise ecclesial function. They have also met with rejection—but not from the institution, which has remained judiciously quiet in this regard. The crisis through which the institutional Church is passing encourages it to see evidence of renewal in the charismatic movements. Yet the charismatic stance has been rejected by self-styled committed Christians—those working to make the Church politically and socially effective. They believe that the charismatic movements represent a turning away from the true problems towards an unhealthy form of mysticism and, most important of all, an unacceptable political *status quo*.

We have no intention of avoiding these questions in this issue of *Concilium*. On the other hand our primary aim is not to take up a specific position in regard to them but to offer the basic information for a responsible consideration of them. The reader must judge the matter for himself on the basis of the data supplied as well as the significant gaps in our knowledge.

Therefore this issue is devoted to the way in which a noninstitutional movement is in fact ecclesially organized: by, that is, the charism, the gift of the Spirit for the evangelical growth of the community. As Dr. Laurentin's article on charismatic language shows, that definition is rather summary. Nevertheless it suffices to delineate the field of our study, which is the historical development of the Church.

A definition of charism remains abstract if it does not arise from the historical movement; in other words charisms have no existence apart from the movements which call themselves charismatic. It seemed necessary to look at the history of these movements in some detail. We intended to look separately at this historical process in a largely chronological and then a more sociological perspective. Unfortunately it proved impossible to find a sociologist to see to the second aspect of the study and we were forced to treat both historical standpoints in a single article. But the result is very effective: Dr. Gerest's very solid article offers fundamental considerations of supreme theological interest.

This long historical survey makes the loss of the planned study of Luke less unfortunate. In spite of constant urging we never received this contribution—an aspect of the hard work that goes into the production of *Concilium* which readers should perhaps be more aware of. Luckily the loss of the intended article was compensated for by three other articles (by Dussel, Sartori and Vidales) which happily complement the historical survey in considering the political and ecclesial consequences of the charismatic movements.

This historical, political and ecclesial emphasis should not obscure the secondary thrust of the articles on discernment and the unpredictability of grace. The question is not easy, for who would claim the right to judge the action of the Spirit? Who in fact is sure that he is acting in accordance with the Spirit? What horizon of action and of thought allows me to say that this or that is of the Spirit? If the horizon in question is the Church, then which Church is in question? The hierarchical, institutional Church? Surely that Church has ultimate right of access to the Spirit? Surely in the end the Holy Office is justified against the prophets? How is it possible to be simultaneously the Church of the Spirit, of whom one never knows whence he comes nor whither he goes, and the institutional Church whose structures outline the future?

This volume closes with testimonies and bulletins. One of these deserves special attention; Dr. Abela's article on liturgy is exceptionally interesting in that he wrote it with considerable freedom without ignoring the underlying historical questions. It seems a firm expression of the emergent desire that lay-people should not be mere 'consumers' in the Church but co-responsible for the forms in which they express their belief or prayer. The questions raised by Dr. Abela are not of interest only to specialists: liturgy is the concern of all Christians.

The articles in this volume will fulfill their aim if they show that the present ready identification of the so-called 'renewal movement' with the 'charismatic' movement is mistaken and conducive of a monopoly within the Church. I cannot seriously deny the presence of charismatics in the renewal movement, but I do refute the notion that the renewal movement has a monopoly of charisms in the present-day world. The Holy Spirit is no one's slave, and the Church is more diverse than such a notion would allow.

CHRISTIAN DUQUOC

PART I

Articles

René Laurentin

Charisms: Terminological Precision

'There is much talk of charisms. But as soon as one approaches the vast literature on the subject one is struck by the lack of precision in the use of the word'.

THIS is B. N. Wambacq's opinion at the beginning of an article where he abandons the attempt to give a definition of the word.[1] I shall try to give some precision to its meaning since it is the title of this number of *Concilium* and any serious discipline should determine the meaning of the words which it uses.

ACCEPTED USES AND MAIN CATEGORIES OF THE WORD CHARISM

I start with the various main categories in which the term is used, beginning with the ordinary and secular use, in order to pin down methodically the scope of its meaning.

1. The word *charism* has only recently and unobtrusively become part of the current vocabulary. In France, Littré and, after him, the dictionaries of the first half of the twentieth century have on the whole ignored it, even the first edition of Robert where the word only appears for the first time in the supplement of 1970, with a quotation from Daniel-Rops's *Histoire Sainte*. The word appears as recently and without attracting attention in the English, German, Italian and other dictionaries. The word is usually referred to the 'religious' and, more specifically, to the Christian vocabulary.

2. Max Weber, who died in 1920, introduced the word into sociology.[2] He distinguished three types of authority: traditional, rational, or charismatic, according to whether it was based on the prestige of the

3

past, the rationale of administration, or the (irrational) inspiration of the leader.

Weber gave the word a strictly sociological acceptation. He was not concerned with the intrinsic nature of the charism nor whether the claim of the charismatic leader was genuine or false. What interested him was that this quality was recognized by the people obeying him and the way in which it functioned socially as a consequence of this. Thus defined, the concept is illuminating and suggestive. It makes it easy to identify the type of charismatic leader, whether in the religious or secular field, from Moses to Mao. For centuries Moses was only followed by charismatic stages, the Judges, until, with Solomon, the administrative and bureaucratic rationale took over. And today one wonders what will follow on Mao Tse-Tung: a charismatic stage, or a Maoist tradition, or the most natural trend: namely, an attempt at rational administrative organization as has happened in the case of other inspired revolutions.

Weber gave this notion a sociological framework. However, he borrowed the word from the apostle Paul *via* the theologian Rudolf Sohm (*Kirchenrecht,* Leipzig, 1898) to whom he referred explicitly (p. 222). Following Moehler, Sohm accepted as a principle that the organization of Christianity was not juridical but charismatic (p. 25).

The meaning Weber gave the word has been largely accepted in sociological writing, particularly among Anglo-Saxon writers, but has not been well received by ethnologists (cf. Michael Hill, *Sociology of Religion,* London, 1975). A number of biblical scholars of the Old Testament talk in this sense of the charismatic king in Israel (e.g., W. Beyerling, 'Das Königscharisma bei Saül', in *ZAW*, 73, 1961, p. 201; Z. Weisman, 'Anointing as a Motif in the Making of the Charismatic King', in *Biblica* 57, 1976, p. 394). These scholars have not taken this word from their source (the word *charisma* does not appear in the Greek version of the Septuagint) but from the construction Weber has put on it. This literary intervention seems to have escaped Wambac in the remark complaining about the confusion of today's speech.

In brief, the uses of the word all derive from one single source, in the full meaning of the word: the New Testament.

3. 'The word . . . was probably coined by St Paul', Wambacq thinks (art. quoted, p. 346), by linking the verb *charizomai* (= to please) with *charis* (= grace). Nevertheless, one finds it, meaning 'present' (free gift) in a variant of *Sirac* 7: 33, in Theodotion's version (ps. 30:22) and in Philo (Leg. Alleg. 3:78, parallel with *dorea*). It appears seventeen times in the New Testament, fourteen times in Romans and 1-2 Corinthians, the other three times in texts written under Pauline influence (I Tim. 4:14; II Tim. 1:6; I Peter 4:10).

The word is used:

in a general way to designate gifts bestowed by God gratuitously (Rom. 1:11; 5:15; 6:23; 11:29; II Cor. 1:11);

more often in an apparently more specific sense in order to designate those gifts which are used for the building up of the Christian community (Rom. 12:6; I Cor. 12:4, 9, 28, 30, 31 with which one could link 1:7 and 7:7; I Tim. 4:14; II Tim. 1:6 and I Peter 4:10). It is in this second sense that the word has become a permanent part of the Christian vocabulary and appears as the title of this present issue.[3]

4. Historically, the word *charism* has tended to suffer an eclipse. What Paul described as charism in I Corinthians, particularly glossolalia, very early on already perturbed and embarrassed the commentators—they didn't know what to make of it because 'this no longer happens in our days', as John Chrysostom ingenuously observes in his Homily 29:12, 1. The word reappears in spiritual movements where the powerful experience of these gifts is periodically rediscovered from within. This happened in the Middle Ages in the wake of Bernard of Clairvaux, Francis of Assisi, Dominic and other not so well accepted spiritual figures, like Joachim of Flora. Thomas Aquinas worked out an organic theology of the charism in the thirteenth century.[4] In the following centuries, however, this concept was pushed into the margin of Catholic theology. The Dominican tradition which developed from Aquinas was for centuries one of the rare places where it was still dealt with. There is no article on charism in the *Dictionnaire de théologie catholique* where the word only occurs again in the indexes (1954).

The basic reason for this marginal treatment is that the emerging of charisms was seen as a danger to the institution: it might confront the established authority with an authority which was beyond control. These fears found historical expression in the Montanist crisis and the problems created by the spiritual groups of the Middle Ages.[5] Cardinal Ruffini, one of the leaders of the minority, expressed them at the Vatican Council. He opposed the recognition of charisms because he saw there a danger of 'disorder'. The texts of Vatican II bear the marks of this underlying tension in the debates. No. 7 of the Constitution *Lumen Gentium* shows that those who drafted the text did not manage to overcome this tension. The conciliar text seems to put side by side and in some way to oppose two kinds of gifts: 'hierarchical[6] and charismatic'. No. 12 avoids this distortion by describing the charisms as 'special graces which make (the faithful) fit to undertake various offices and tasks advantageous for the renewal and upbuilding of the Church' (Abbott and Gallagher's translation). This normally includes the functions of authority in accordance with the pastoral epistles where the ordained ministry of the leader of the community is described as a charism (I Tim. 4:14; II Tim. 11:7). Once past the obstacle of the basic debate on the Church the conciliar vocabulary[7] finds a better balance, particularly in the Decree on the Apostolate of the Laity (no. 3, par. 3).

The core of the problem is this: in theory there can only be harmony between charisms and the legitimate authority since the latter also proceeds from the Spirit and is normally supported by a charism. The trinitarian presentation of I Cor. 12:4 suggests that the *forces* (*energemata*) which originate from the Father emerge in the form of *charisms* (*charismata*) of the Spirit, and take the form of ministries, referred to Christ, and they include the apostolic ministry. But in fact and in history human weakness and sin introduce disharmony, either because charisms deviate and flourish in disorder (I Cor. 14) or because authority sets itself up externally in the way of the powers of this world. Wherever the conflict comes into the open and degenerates into mutual accusation, there will be escalation and radical stances which harm the Church's balance and vitality.

AN ATTEMPTED DEFINITION

We have now reached the starting-point for a definition. The attempt implies a relativity and we have to see where it lies.

It is not strictly necessary to use the word itself. Paul himself has used other terms and does not always use it when he speaks of those gifts which God has bestowed for the service and the building up of the community.

Nevertheless, it is the most obvious word and best borne out in the description of rather well-specified phenomena. If it is adopted, it is better to use it with clarity and methodically. It is precisely the function of theology (*fides quaerens intellectum*) to put into order and illuminate the data of faith:—the sources of revelation, and primarily Scripture;—the life of the Church where this revelation is lived in history and in the actual present.

The texts of the New Testament themselves refer to a personal and communal experience. They have kept a provocative value throughout the centuries, including the Council. I shall therefore not limit myself to a simple archaeological analysis of the language. What is important in this issue concerned with spirituality is to recapture the way in which God's gift is lived, manifest and operational, yesterday and today, not without a historical evolution of both terms and meaning. Thomas Aquinas was right in describing theology as the science of salvation: not only *in theory* but also *in practice*. In other words, it is, in modern parlance, a *praxis:* i.e., a knowledge which actively works out its object in human and social reality: here the reality of the Church as the body of Christ. There is therefore some tension between the witness of the sources and the actuality which has to be illuminated and orientated, as Thomas Aquinas knew so admirably to do in his day.

In the New Testament there are eight lists of these gifts intended for a function to be fulfilled in the community:—four using the word *charism* explicitly: I Cor. 12:4–10; 12:28–31; Rom. 12:6–8; I Peter 4:10;—four without this word: I Cor. 14:6–13; I Cor. 14:26; Eph. 4:11; Mk. 16, 17–18. And from this point on one should look at the numerous texts of the New Testament which provide evidence of these gifts, above all the Acts of the Apostles.

There is in St Paul,[8] as after him, a groping towards an adjustment of the signifying to the signified.

Negative precisions

Starting with the data provided by the Bible, history and the present, it is important first of all to eliminate a certain amount of confusion by stating clearly what charisms are not (or, at least, not essentially).

1. They are not the prerogative of the primitive communities. They do not belong to a past that is over and done with. They belong to the permanence of the Church as confirmed by Vatican II when it used an interpretation of St Paul in opposition to a decadent tradition.

2. Nor are they privileges reserved to certain individuals. All Christians may receive and use these gifts for the building up of the community, according to the same teaching of St Paul and Vatican II.

3. The charisms are *not extraordinary* gifts. They belong to the ordinary way in which the gift of God works in the life of the Church. One has to beware of the illusory attempt to define them by exceptional or striking characteristics, even if it is in their nature to be visible and to stimulate hope. Even in the matter of glossolalia or cures, what is extraordinary is not essential to the charisms, and what is essential to them is not extraordinary.

4. They are *not ecstatic* gifts. It is through some rather gratuitous extra-biblical assimilations that this characteristic is attributed to some of them, particularly to speaking with tongues. 'The spirits of the prophets (and the other charismatic individuals) are subject to the prophets', according to I Cor. 14:32.

5. If the charisms may be said to be 'supernatural' in the sense that they are free gifts of the Spirit, it is only on condition that 'supernatural' is not understood as superadded to nature, like a kind of superstructure, a metal crown on a bodily head. The charism sets free natural gifts according to the diversity of people and of the human

communities. Hence charisms touch the whole of human reality, individually and collectively, the body and the psychical features, according to the diversity of commitment or involvement.[9]

6. They do not constitute a uniform and fixed group, nor even a closed order. They are of infinite diversity according to the needs of the Church and the historical and geographical diversity of the situation.

7. They are *nothing without the charity* within which they have to operate.

DEFINITION

Taking account of the harmony of the structures and the diversity to which St Paul, history and modern experience bear witness, one may propose the following definition: *Charisms are free gifts of the Spirit intended for the building up of the Church, the Body of Christ.*

Concentrating on the exact meaning of the terms involved we find that:

'Charisma' may be translated by *free gift* because it is a word derived from *charis* which means grace, with the suffix *ma* which adds the nuance expressing the perfect of a verb: the action as carried through and completed. Paul puts *charisma* (attributed to the Spirit) on a parallel with *energema* (not *energia*) which he attributes to the Father. The root *charis* also connotes joy, according to the etymology of the corresponding verb *charizomaï* which is linked with *charis, grace,* and *chara, joy,* the joy of an harmonious setting free of forces of the individual for the service of God.

At the level of psychological analysis, Antoine Vergote presents this aspect of the charism with a carefully amended reference to the Freudian categories of desire and pleasure: a spirituality centred on the Spirit has the capacity to receive and sanctify men's affective powers, including the subconscious ones, by directing them towards God because: 'God manifests himself by an increase of desire and enjoyment. This wards off the dark powers which might obstruct man in an insuperable conflict . . . The gifts of the Spirit of which the charismatic movements avail themselves show at what depth the Spirit can accord with the human mind. What seems to us essential to these movements is that they create the space and the climate of confidence for spontaneous and joyful prayer' ('L'expérience de l'Esprit', in *Mélanges Schillebeeckx,* Paris, 1976, pp. 221–3).

I have said that these gifts proceed from the Spirit because I Cor. 12:4–11 strongly insists on this. It is true that A. Chevallier has emphasized that Rom. 12:4 and Peter 4:10 speak of charisms without specific reference to the Holy Spirit. In his view Paul chose the word *charismata* in order to replace the word *pneumatika,* used by the

Corinthians (cf. I Cor. 12, 1) and stressing in-spiration while *charismata* helped him to put the accent back on the gratuitousness on God's part and the usefulness for the Church.

But if we look at what Paul had in mind: to restore the freedom of the Spirit and the overflowing of in-spiration for the functional service of the community, it is clear that, through the centuries, all those who experienced these gifts attributed them to the Spirit with constant reference to I Cor. 12:1–11.

We have to deal here with an experience wrapped in the anonymity and discretion which correspond to the use of a neutral word to indicate the Spirit: *To Pneuma* in the Greek of the New Testament. But the fact that John always treats this (neutral) *Pneuma* as masculine: That one (*ekeinos,* masculine demonstrative pronoun, John 14:26; 15:26; 16, 8, 13, 14), and describes him as an 'other Paraclete' (Christ being the first Paraclete), and, finally, numerous converging data from Scripture and experience induce us to recognize that he is a Person[10] as well as a 'fountain of living waters for eternal life' (John 7:38–9), and a liberating force (*dynamis*) according to Luke and Paul. One cannot stress enough the *mysterious* modalities of this experience of the Spirit.

Lastly, these charismatic gifts (as distinct from the gifts of mysticism) are meant for the building up of the community. By taking a rigid line on this aspect, classical theology saw the charisms as useful for the Church but not for the charismatic individual. In fact the building up of the community is in a vital sense inseparable from that of the individual. No doubt, the charism has an altruistic character, sometimes going so far as to laying down one's life for the sake of others. But even in this case it shows itself as the diffusion and overspill of what builds up the charismatic individual himself, quite specifically, as the living cell or organ of the Church. In this sense the charisms are slanted towards roles, functions and ministries. At a deeper level they are *Agape* operating in the one Spirit (I Cor. 12). What is too limited in the position of classical theology in its exclusion of the charismatic individual can be amended by referring to the authority of Paul himself where he says that the speaking of tongues is a gift aiming at the building up of the individual who speaks: 'He who speaks in a tongue edifies himself'[11] (I Cor. 14:4) which is more clearly borne out by experience today.

AN ATTEMPTED CLASSIFICATION

In order to account for the diversity which underlies the use of this word in Scripture, classical theology and experience, one may attempt a typology or classification of the charisms in the light of the definition proposed above.

1. The charisms show in the most obvious way the gifts through which the Spirit structures the Church by rousing from within the services and functions of the community according to the diversity and qualities of each member. In this perspective there is no opposition between charism and institution. A ministry is normally the expression of a charism and a permanent charism takes the form of a ministry or service (I Cor. 12:4).

There is an infinite variety of charisms. In the order of time there are first the basic charisms such as the inspiration of the sacred authors of the Bible and the apostolate of the Twelve. After that we have the gifts of interpretation (scribes, exegetes, commentators). The charisms can refer to the function of worship, the word and government. To these three interrelated branches one can link a whole flowering of gifts concerning respectively:

(a) prayer in all its forms;

(b) the charisms of the word: prophets, men of learning, catechists, preachers, etc., and all those charisms that are connected with education and training;

(c) those that have as their object authority or presidency, but also the social organization of the Church, mutual aid, charity, without forgetting discernment.

2. Since charisms are defined by their end, which is the building up of the community, this word is convenient to indicate the gifts which inspire the choice and implementation of the state of life: marriage and celibacy, as Paul himself suggests in I Cor. 7:7. The charisms vary according to the different ways of life: eremitical, cenobitical, and so on, including the new forms where married and celibate Christians live together in one community, occasionally of the monastic kind.

3. Lastly, the concept of charism fits the sacramental character of baptism, confirmation and holy orders, which define the insertion into the Church, body of Christ, and its basic organic functions. What is important is that these gratuitous gifts proceed from the freedom of the Spirit operating within the freedom of the individual. More important still is the fact that their value is not measured by the intensity of the inspiration nor by the striking features of what they produce but by the charity (I Cor. 13:1–3) which is their measure and their strength through the one Spirit which works all in all. Lastly, it is important that they are thus integrated in an organic (and therefore dynamic and ordered) way in the Church, body of Christ.

Translated by Theo Weston

Notes

1. B. N. Wambacq, 'Le mot charisme', in *Nouvelle revue théologique* 97 (1975), pp. 345–55.
2. Max Weber (1864–1920), *Wirtschaft und Gesellschaft* (posthumous, 1921), ch. 3, para. 4.
3. The religious concept is also used in the art. 'Charisma' in the *Lexikon der Pädagogik* (Freiburg, 1952) I, pp. 621–622 which suggests that one can attribute the charism of education to Dom Bosco: here, too, there are religious overtones. Looking through a number of dictionaries in several libraries I have mostly found nothing at all. The word appears in very recent and relatively obscure publications apart from the sociological dictionaries which always return to Max Weber, such as Georges Thinès and A. Lempereur, *Dictionnaire général des sciences humaines* (Paris, 1975), pp. 171–172.
4. Thomas Aquinas, *Summa theologica*, I–II, qu. 3, art. 1 and especially II–II, qu. 171–178. J. V. M. Pollet's article, 'Les charismes' in *Initiation théologique* (Paris, 1952), vol. 3, pp. 1081–1108, shows how far this question had vanished from the theological horizon in the first decades of this century.
5. History seems to have treated spiritual groups with excessive severity: R. Laurentin, *Pentecôtisme chez les catholiques* (Paris, 1974), ch. 6, pp. 169–86.
6. This word 'hierarchical' is unfortunate when used to describe authority (*exousia*) which, in the New Testament, has a typically non-hierarchical character, based as it is on the image of the Servant and not on that of those who exercise the power of domination among the pagans (Luke 22:25–7; John 13:4–15, and so on).
7. The Council texts use 'charisma' eleven times and 'charismaticus' (already used by Pius XII in his *Mystici Corporis*) three times. These uses are listed in P. Delhaye's *Concilium Vaticanum II, Concordance, Index, Liste de fréquence, Tables comparatives* (Louvain, 1974). See *Lumen Gentium* 4, 12, 25, 30.
8. M. A. Chevallier, *Esprit de Dieu, parole d'homme* (Neuchâtel, 1966), followed by D. W. B. Robinson, 'Charismata versus pneumatica', in *The Reformed Theological Review* 31 (1972), pp. 49–55, E. Cothenet, in *SDB* 8, pp. 1287–303, J. Herten, 'Charisma', in J. Hainz, *Kirche im Werden* (Munich, 1976), pp. 57–89, dispute the current interpretation of *charisma* in Paul, in the technical sense of later theology, as do Kittel's *Dictionary*, H. Küng, J. Ratzinger and the TOB. It is true that occasionally Paul's use is open to various interpretations from which one has to choose in order to arrive at a definition.
9. B. Lepesant *Dynamique de group et conversion charismatique* (Paris, 1976), makes a judicious comparison between the experience of a charismatic group and a case of group dynamics: the same psychological means are differently orientated. On another essentially theological basis H. Mühlen joins this analysis, taking the charisms as 'natural gifts set free by the holy Spirit': *Die Erneuerung des christlichen Glaubens, Charisma, Geistbefreiung* (Munich, 1974), ch. 5, p. 235: 'A natural gift which is set free and used by the holy Spirit for the building up and growth of the body of Christ'.
10. Council of Constantinople (381), Denzinger-Schönmetzer, no. 150.

11. Experience suggests that we should maintain the positive and obvious sense of Paul's text: 'He who speaks in a tongue edifies himself' (I Cor. 14:4) rather than interpret it in a negative sense, as classical theology tends to do: 'One does not edify oneself' (I Cor. 14:4f), 'one only edifies the community' (X. Léon-Dufour, *Dictionnaire du Nouveau Testament,* Paris, 1975, p. 220).

12. The edification of the Church by the action and internal structuring of the Spirit was brought to light again by J. A. Moehler (Tübingen, 1824). The same line of thought was pursued by Hans Küng in his *The Church,* 1968, vol. I, ch. 2, 3, 'Charismatic structure', and G. Hasenhüttl, *Charisma, Ordnungsprinzip der Kirche* (Freiburg 1970). On this principle of classification, see Sr Jeanne d'Arc, 'Panorama des charismes', in *Vie spirituelle* 129 (1975), pp. 503–22.

Claude Gérest

The Hour of Charisms: The Development of the Charismatic Movements in America

ONE cannot refer to charismatic movements in the plural as a matter of course. I would not like it to be thought that in doing so I have mastered a typology, when apart from Pentecostalism and neo-Pentecostalism I am not sure that there have been any 'charismatic' movements properly so called. I would like to avoid the trap of searching for spiritual links with great forebears, or, on the contrary, with compromising precedents.

I assume continuity between Catholic neo-Pentecostalism and twentieth-century Protestant Pentecostalism, as also between the latter and the American 'revivalism' of the nineteenth century. This continuity can be traced, and its reality is acknowledged (even when qualified in the process). I will therefore treat of these three spiritual experiences as of a single history in three stages, each one appealing to and sometimes criticising the others.

As we pass from one group to another, we will inevitably notice variations both in sociological composition and in theology; variations which should be looked at in the light of shifts in the historical context. No one, least of all any theologian today, has any doubt that a certain degree of dependence exists between religious phenomena and economic and cultural situations. The connexion thus established is illuminating: we are better able to see the scenario within which the event emerges; but does this mean that we have any better grasp of its specific quality? That we really know why it has emerged? I leave the reader to give his own answer, being tempted to make my own Paul Veyne's pithy assessment: 'Can the French Revolution be explained scientifically? No, or at least no more than the *département* Loir et Cher can. At all events, sociological studies on Pentecostalism do not currently appear to have got beyond the stage of judicious comparisons. They enable one to understand what it is that makes the milieux concerned accept the message; they do not induce one to consider that message as a product of the milieu.[1]

The reader must expect nothing here, therefore, but an historical description with no claim to be an analysis.

The article by René Laurentin elsewhere in this issue will have put us right, if that were necessary, as regards the meanings of the word 'charismatic'. In this historical description, I am taking it in its narrowest and most precise sense: that which concerns the gifts of the Spirit for the edification of the community—gifts which are most frequently 'manifestations of power' (speaking in tongues, prophecy, healing), but which are also the various abilities for fulfilling the tasks necessary to the common life. A wider meaning of the word, based on its etymology, should not, however, be lost sight of: moved by grace and in the joy of the Spirit. Attention to charisms is an integral part of any dynamic process of rediscovery of the active intervention of God.

FIRST STAGE: AMERICAN REVIVALISM, CONVERSION AND HOLINESS

Conversion

(*a*) People of the 'frontier' and 'revivalism'

The United States, in the first half of the 19th century, served as an arena for the most daring experiments. At the religious level the rejection of any offical religion by the Constitution, the arrival of emigrants belonging to all the Christian denominations, and the new type of American man enabled Protestantism to develop its potentialities in a way that, until then, it had done nowhere else. In the towns and villages of New England, the influence of the churches was not yet what it would be at the end of the century; but the acceptance of the newcomers into the parishes, where they found that a good deal of the cultural life of their countries of origin had been integrated into the national life of the country of their adoption, made Christianity, in spite of the neutrality of the State, act as a cement for American unity. Protestantism emerged as one of the fundamental elements of the New World. It would not be long before people would attribute their blessed prosperity to the independence of mind, the taste for adventure, and the other virtues developed by the Reformation. Balancing this, there was an entire Christian literature treating of American 'Messianism'.

Whereas the towns provided the churches of European origin (Episcopalian, Methodist, Baptist, Presbyterian) with the means of spreading their network of parishes, the 'frontier' lent itself to more original experiments. By 'frontier' was meant the western limit of the central and southern states, land still given over to agricultural colonization. There a population of pioneers lived a mobile, rough and often violent life. The small proprietors ('plain folk') were poor, and threatened in their livelihood, but not without hope of growing richer; they felt they had a great deal to struggle against in nature, in their neighbours' greed or in their own weaknesses, but not so much in the economic structures. As a social class they were as different from the workers of New England as the big planters and slave-owners. In these scattered surroundings, where one was far more cut off from European traditions than in the rest of the country, religious life oscillated between gross indifference, coupled with a high degree of moral anarchy, and aspirations towards a 'muscular Christianity', according to the curiously modern expression of the revivalist, Al Campbell, who in 1827 founded the Disciples of Christ. Corresponding to its geographical situation and its socio-psychological characteristics, the 'frontier' was to have its own particular form of religious assembly: the 'revival' campaign and the 'camp meeting'.

The 'revival' was not an invention of nineteenth-century America; they were known in the eighteenth century, in both 'worlds'. This however does not make it any the less a typical expression of United States Protestantism. As it is more important to picture a revival to oneself than to try and define it, let us listen to a witness to the Cane Ridge assemblies, which were the point of departure for the 'great western revival' in 1801: 'These assemblies are made up for the most part of plain, passionate sermons to which the audience responded with wailing, sobs and cries. As long as the preacher's voice was uppermost, order (a relative order, it is true) reigned in the assembly. But the moment his voice became submerged by the great voice of a people in distress, all exterior order broke down, and the general emotion burst forth on all sides. Each one raised his voice in anguish: here a sinner, overwhelmed by his guilt, asked pardon of God; there another, relieved of the burden of his sins, gave thanks to the divine mercy; elsewhere Christians exhorted their as yet unconverted relatives and friends to repent, while the pastors, the natural leaders of the movement, left the platform to pass on, row by row, their exhortations and their prayers. The most diverse scenes met the spectators' gaze, in so far as there could be any spectators there who did not soon, in spite of themselves, become actors in this great drama. One man, driven by the obsessions of an awakened conscience, tried to flee the camp, and soon fell, stopped short by the sovereign hand of God. Another passed, almost without transition, from blasphemy to prayers. From the midst of all this disturbance rose isolated groups of chanting of an incomparable sweetness, the natural expression of renewed sentiments'.[2]

(b) Community organization of 'revivalism'

This kind of assembly reminds one of the 'mission' which has been so fashionable in French Catholicism since the eighteenth century, with slightly more emotional emphasis. There is, however, a great difference between 'missions' and 'revivals'. The former are planned programmed and directed from above, that is to say by the competent ecclesiatical authorities (bishops, interdiocesan services, religious orders). The 'revivals' came from the grass-roots or at least the original American 'revivals' did—and they usually began with the heightening of religious feeling in one individual or a restricted group, which then sought to affect others in the same way. The role of lay people, including women and children was of prime importance.

This initial spontaneity—which in any case was sometimes inspired by models—soon gave rise to a certain degree of organization, if only in order to carry through the campaigns for evangelization. The organization was variously based within the established churches or in the new communities. 'Revivalist' Christians attached themselves more or less closely to the different denominations, showed a moderate interest in them and practised among themselves an ecumenism which benefited from their lack of theological knowledge. But they called on or were offered the aid of the churches as ministers of the word, although lay preachers were also beginning to emerge. The most celebrated 're-vivalists' were pastors like the Presbyterian MacGee (late eighteenth and early nineteenth centuries) and Charles G. Finney (1792–1875), a Congregationalist of Presbyterian origin. Many of them got into difficulties with the authorities in their respective churches—of which they distorted the teaching, tarnished the 'respectability' with their over-excited style and denounced the lukewarmness. In the second half of the century, preachers of 'revivals' were even more independent of the traditional churches, as was Dwight Moody (1837–1899), for example, or Robert P. Smith (1827–1899).

'Revivalism' worked in favour of the churches—with one exception, the Methodist Church. There is nothing surprising about this, when one recalls its origins. Wesley (1703–1791), the inspiration behind Methodism, wished throughout his life not to found a new denomination but to put new life into Anglicanism through 'conversion' campaigns; he was one of the greatest revivalists of all time. An ardent preacher and a man of method, he reached thousands of listeners in his open-air sermons, grouped those who were persuaded into 'classes' (of about fifteen men or women) and 'societies' (according to the pattern of the neighbourhood), which were a cross between a school and a club or Masonic lodge, and placed them under the surveillance of a leader; he chose numerous preachers from among the gifted lay people, divided them into 'circuits' or 'districts' which corresponded in a way to the provinces of the mendicant orders in the Catholic Church (with assemblies which resembled chapters). This communitarian structure left a great deal of the responsibility with the grass-roots, according the Protestant principle of the 'universal' priesthood, and gave wide scope to the authority of the 'charismatic' leader in the exercise of his authority and the influence he had on those he had converted. When Methodism changed from being a network of brotherhoods within the Anglican Church to being an autonomous church, its organization, which was centered on the evangelization campaign, did not change much. In England, as is well known, the transition occurred after Wesley's death, but in the United States it took place in 1784, because of Independence. The Methodist Episcopal Church (MEC) established its autonomy in relation to the American Episcopalian Church as well as in relation to metropolitan Methodism. The assembly of its preachers placed a bishop at its head, which was a source of displeasure to Wesley. The new denomination was closely associated with the 'frontier' and with 'revivalism'. One of its characteristic institutions was the 'camp meeting', a gathering at the edge of the forest to which thousands of country families came once the harvest was over. Fruit of the initiative of the faithful, and only tolerated by the church authorities, these prayer meetings served also as impromptu villages, markets and kermesses, though they were essentially occasions for evangelization and conversion.[3]

Responsive to spontaneity, to encounter and to understanding worked out in common in a concrete situation, these people of the revival were not predisposed to accept the big institutions. They were, more than once, sources of dissidence, even within Methodism, however suited to them it might be. Among the best-known American sects, the Adventists (in 1831) and the Mormons (in 1834) began life with an exodus from the world and the churches which, in one important respect, was a revival: a revival which gained added excitement from the announcement of the end of the world. However, whereas classical revivalism adhered to a strict biblical orthodoxy, the members of the new sects[4] were inspired by the revelations or discoveries of Miller and Smith, whom they ranked on a par with the prophets of

...

...

Scripture. One can therefore give them their place in the line of those who, from Wesley to Pentecostalism, aimed to actualize the biblical message, not to complete it. There were other dissidents, on the other hand, who were simply revivalists who had not been able or willing to organize their lives as converts within the churches from which they came thus the Christians (1806), the United Brothers of Christ (1808) or the Disciples of Christ emerged from regroupings which dated from the great revival of the west in the early nineteenth century. The latter, who had a certain numerical importance, pushed several of the 'frontier' tendencies to the extreme: Christian anticlericalism through rejection of a professional ministry, anti-intellectual 'fundamentalism' through a desire to have no other confession of faith but the Bible, insistence on conversion through refusal of baptism for infants.

This last point, this 'baptist' tendency, the determining influence of which in the social composition of a religious group is plain to see, fell within the logical framework of 'revivalism' and Methodism. Wesley in particular spoke and acted as though the 'simple' baptized, as long as he had not gone through the experience of conversion was outside 'salvation'; but he was too steeped in Anglican tradition to refuse baptism to infants. The dissident American groups, in short, did what he had not dared to do. To reserve baptism and entry into their ranks to fully aware, decided adults was to suggest that conversion was not just a goal to be aimed at but an absolutely fundamental principle of the Christian community.

(c) What kind of conversion?

With its Christian regime and its morality based on the harmonious development of all the virtues, the Catholic Middle Ages had effectively put to one side the biblical theme of conversion (that was the business of monks and 'penitents'). Luther brought it back to the centre of life and theology, at the same time as he treated it in function of his own sutuation. A convert, such as himself, did not pass from unbelief to belief, still less from vice to virtue, but from the pharisaism of 'justification through works' to abandonment to God, in faith, of all concern for one's salvation. From then on the convert was, above all, one who believed and who regarded himself as the object of the gratuitous choice of the all-merciful God.

American revivalism inherited this Lutheranism via the Pietists, the Moravians and the Methodists. One sociologist, Bryan Wilson, speaks in this connexion of "conversionist" movements.[5] And conversion, above all when sought for, is an illustration of 'justification by faith', the great principle of the Reformation. To become converted was to allow oneself to be converted. 'Acceptance of the salvation of God who has prepared everything' was the first thing that had to be learnt. Now the one who thus instructs those who would 'first become better through their own strength', and through doing so 'recommend themselves to the Divine Mercy', is no other than Finney, one of the revivalists most steeped in pragmatism and moralism; and he adds: it is impossible that they should become even slightly better until they achieve the one thing God is asking of them, total abandonment'.[6]

Revivalist preaching stressed the 'felt', 'lived' character of conversion. Luther could say that he came to the experience (*Erlebnis*) of mercy through the anguish and the joys of deliverance; but he did not make the process of his own conversion the norm for the community. The one idea the revivalists had was to precipitate sudden conversions, marking in a life a before and an after, of which one could give an account to one's 'brothers' (are you converted? they would ask one another).

If, according to the principle of justification by faith, they continued faithfully to affirm the gratuitous nature of conversion, the revivalists did not draw from it all the consequences that the Reformers drew from it. Calvinistic predestination was very far removed from their spirit and practice (it provided the unconverted with such a good excuse!) The Moravian brethren were already reproaching Wesley for his lack of Protestant orthodoxy; many Presbyterian pastors not unreasonably regarded Finney and Moody as supporters of 'Arminianism' (that is to say, of that Dutch doctrine within the Reformation movement which made predestination dependant on a prevision of the Fall). Revivalism in fact preached on the relationship between freedom and grace in the light of the Catholic concept of *synergia* (man's energy operating within the sphere of God's and in collaboration with it). 'Some months ago', wrote Finney, 'a treatise appeared on "Regeneration, effect of Divine Power". In it the author proves that this work is acomplished by the Spirit of God, at which point he stops. Now, it would have been equally true, philosophically and scripturally speaking, to say that conversion is the work of man. The writer therefore only demonstrated half of the truth'.[7] These disputes about predestination and the enslaved will, points of doctrine carefully adhered to in Protestant orthodoxy at the beginning of the nineteenth century, were introduced here in the name, not of theological liberalism but of missionary experience.

Generally speaking, conversion in American revivalism meant the conversion of ordinary men and women, those who came together at the camp-meeting. They had no great sense of having been pharisees, clinging to their own righteousness (although they were warned not to be); they were acutely conscious that they had been blasphemers, alcoholics, quarrellers, and lovers of all sorts of frivolity. For them conversion remained a religious drama, a struggle between God and Satan, with strong moralistic overtones.[8] The morality of the converted was a Puritan morality, especially among the Disciples of Christ, who even forbade themselves dancing and card games; it has been noted that this Puritanism was an aid to survival and often to prosperity at the frontier. Strictness of morals in private life was more or less stressed according to different times and places, but it did not cause as much trouble as did questions of political morality, such as the abolition of slavery, which provoked a schism within the Methodist churches in 1843.[9]

(d) Conversion, emotion, and frontier civilization

In the revivalist milieu, it was above all things important that conversion should be provoked (although it came from God) and also that it should be recognized—recognized by the convert, since it must be a felt experience, and recognized by the assembly, since it was the sociological basis of the latter. Recognition was given, according to one whole Protestant and mystical tradition, by the interior testimony of the Holy Spirit.[10] It was produced also in and through all manner of emotional manifestations. The less alarming of these were tears, cries of joy and excessive enthusiasm. But there were stranger varieties: cataleptic seizures, barking, convulsions and falling about (there is much talk of 'holy rollers').

These phenomena discredited revivalism both inside and outside the churches. Revivalist preachers who, like Finney, reflected on their own activity, rather justified themselves than boasted of having provoked this exacerbated sensibility. Like St Teresa of Avila before them, they knew that bodily manifestations of spirtual experience are more a proof of the weakness of man than of the power of the Spirit. In his *Discourse on Religious Revivals,* the work in which Finney brings together, not without insight, the results of his own experience, we read: 'One of the things which definitely prevents people from desiring religious renewal and working towards it is the fact of the excesses or abuses which have sometimes accompanied strong religious arousal'.[11]

While wishing to safeguard the revival campaigns from certain emotional excesses, Finney profoundly believed that 'God has seen fit to make use of the faculty men have of being aroused in their feelings to produce within them the shock which is almost always needed to lead them to obedience'.[12] We must now see whether he was right or wrong.

What strikes one in this first instance is the extent to which his remark throws light on the conditions of evangelization in the frontier lands. The religious indifference of many listeners had its source not in any previously held ideological position but in a lack of practical interest, out of which they could be shaken by the emotional shock; the individualism which is a reflection of the (rural) social situation renders people more sensitive to a resounding call to the salvation that is offered to each one; Puritan moralism fitted in well with this insecure climate of violence and excess; and finally, while, where there was printing, early Protestantism taught its adherents to read and reflect, the camp meeting provided a channel of expression for those whose capacity for reading and intellectual discussion was limited.

Holiness and Baptism of the Spirit

The masters of 'revivalism' learned to distrust any conversion that took place in an over-emotional climate. Perseverance in the good life—their criteria had become very moralistic—was not always in evidence. They came to regard conversion simply as a first stage or, in their own terms, a 'blessing', which should normally be followed by a second in order to ensure that steadfastness in the surrender to grace which was not achieved in the first. This 'second blessing' was likewise an abrupt, identifiable experience, and was given the name of 'sanctification'.

'Sanctification' was a good Reformation word. By it, Luther meant the fructification of the works of faith and charity through the 'power of the Word' in the converted soul.[13] He took great care to distinguish it from justification: so that no one should imagine himself saved by any other holiness than that of Christ, sanctification was placed after salvation, as one of its consequences. But it was in no way a second encounter with Grace. Thus the orthodox Protestants did not recognize themselves in the teaching of Wesley or, later, in that of the American revivalists on the two 'blessings'. They were all the more opposed to it in that the father of Methodism aspired to a state of holiness in which the soul was 'purged' of all sin and without connivance with temptation.[14] This 'perfectionism'—a word often used in dispute against the people of the 'revival'—effectively contradicted the Lutheran affirmation of *simul justus et peccator* (the persistence of sin, in the form of concupiscence, in the life of the just).

'Sanctification' was the object of passionate debates between revivalists and churchmen hostile to revivals. It was not accepted by all revivalists, amongst whom the Calvinist influence remained strong. Finney, Torrey and Moody, however, although they were not Methodists, preached 'holiness'. It was part of the logic of revivalism, of its desire for spiritual experiences, for verification through the moral process of an authentic conversion. It undoubtedly suited the American optimism of a world that was expanding (a milieu which willingly accepted from Protestantism the appeal to individual responsibility, but had little appreciation of the pessimism which imposed limits on perfection). Besides, the American revivalists painted a more modest picture of holiness than did the Wesleyans, and they linked it closely to missionary work. It was given, when one asked in prayer, because one accepted (freely) 'baptism in the Spirit' or 'clothing with power from on high'.

Baptism of the Spirit in American Revivalism

The masters of revivalism, of whom I have spoken, had no doubt that a new Pentecost was being prepared for their thousands of listeners, that it had already taken place for 'Christians of every category, young converts, people who had professed their religious belief for a long time, ministers, lay people, women, young and old, persons of all degrees of human culture'. It was an event in their life. 'It is not something', wrote Finney, 'in which one can grow gradually by training oneself to accept persuasion and change one's course. It is a gift, an anointing received instantaneously, which can be increased or diminished according to whether he who receives it makes use of it more or less energetically and faithfully for the purpose for which it was given. It is frequently possessed and then lost; or else its manifestation is hindered by something which extinguishes the light of the Holy Spirit in the soul'.[15]

For Torrey, writing in about 1850, as for Finney, the purpose of 'baptism of the Spirit' was 'to prepare us, to equip us for the service of God'. It was to be understood however in line with an experience of 'sanctification', of 'second blessing', distinct from and complementary to conversion. Baptism is preceded by 'a total abandonment of our own will, a complete surrender into the hands of Christ'.[16] And according to Finney, 'as soon as the apostles understood that there was a baptism of the Spirit which they had to await', they must have renounced absolutely all idea of living for themselves in any way whatever and consecrated themselves, with all their strength, to the task ahead of them. This consecration of themselves to the work, this self-denial, this death to all that the world had to offer them, must, in the nature of things, have preceded the intelligent search for 'clothing with power from on high'.[15]

What Finney calls variously 'clothing with power from on high', 'consecration', and 'baptism of the Spirit', is not, like conversion, necessary for the salvation of the individual, but for the mission of the Church; and it is important that communities should urge all their members, without exception, to this fulness of service. Each Christian, he believed, 'has a share of the Spirit of Christ'; this share should, if he is faithful, lead him 'to persevere in prayer until he receives power from on high'.[15] In the revivalist groups of that period, no rite or gesture (such as the imposition of hands) signified this mysterious baptism, which did not enter into competition with baptism of water.[17] It remained an altogether interior reality, verifiable only by its apostolic fruits. It is perceptible to the soul because (normally) the Christian who is clothed with power knows himself to be consecrated and strengthened.[18] But unlike certain followers of Wesley, Finney is reserved about the psychological or psychosomatic signs which tell the believer of his 'consecration'.

The present argument, following the sources, has had little to say about the Holy Spirit as he is conceived of in the revivals. The fact is that the revivalists are not experts in trinitarian theology. Their writings are, in the main, faithful to the churches' major confessions of faith; it was only later that some of them spoke in modalist terms of Christ and the Spirit.[19] Attributing personal sanctification and missionary service to the action of the third person, their praxis was faithful to the scriptural tradition: the Spirit gives assurance of the presence of Jesus in the believer, gives actuality to his Gospel, builds up the ecclesial body and opens up the impossible way to the future of God.

The Holiness Movements in the Second Half of the Nineteenth Century

The search for 'sanctification' and for the second blessing brought the faithful together in prayer meetings, which were fairly numerous during the 1830s. There Protestants of different denominations (Presbyterians, Quakers and so on) met up with the Methodists, the original holders of the doctrine of holiness. These assemblies and revivalist campaigns led to the creation—initially without a break with the churches—of the National Holiness Association (1876). The ecclesiastical authorities mistrusted this organization with its confused ecumenism, the exuberance of which seemed to turn into spiritual anarchy. In 1894 Methodism condemned the organization, the holiness groups became autonomous churches, the best known being the Pilgrim Holiness Church and the Church of the Nazarene. Thus was concluded a whole process which made of the Christian community a community of holiness (and no longer a community centerd upon the signs and means of holiness).

The holiness movements should, by and large, be understood as a violent reaction of the early revivalist milieux of the frontier to the evolution of American Christianity—Methodism included—in the second half of the nineteenth century. It was a reaction in favour of free prayer as opposed to a too rigid form of worship; a Puritan reaction against the surrounding permissiveness (holiness forbade itself all alcohol and entertainment and questioned the legitimacy of tobacco); a fundamentalist reaction against the invasion of theology from Germany, which was hypercritical and open to the appeal of Modernism. These religious tendencies, which sought to maintain the fervour of the camp meeting in the face of a Christianity that adapted itself too well to the world, were to found above all among the agricultural populations of the south and middle west who were benefiting little from the country's generally expanding economy and were threatened as regards the maintenance of their own way of life.

The assembly for free prayer and the bible school were among the most characteristic institutions of the holiness movements. They rejected too much organization, though at the same time wishing to preserve some way of experiencing together conversion, baptism in the spirit and all that followed from it. Fervour and external manifestations played an important role, but none of these manifestations was privileged or regarded as the seal of the Spirit and authentification of a person's consecration. It was this latter point that was to distinguish and sometimes oppose the holiness churches and the Pentecostalism of which we are going to speak.

SECOND STAGE: PENTECOSTALISM AFTER 1900

The Origin of the Pentecostal Churches

Those who first underwent the Pentecostal experience and were instrumental in spreading it, did not all come from the holiness movements or from Methodism. Many did, however, and the rest committed themselves to a venture in which the search for and acceptance of the 'second blessing' belonged, at the least, to its prehistory.[20] This of course, is the point of view of an historian; it goes without saying that the Pentecostalists lived what they lived with the sense of beginning something new, with the Pentecost of the apostolic times as the only point of reference.

At the beginning there was a bible school at Topeka, Kansas. In this school they were familiar with no other book but the Book, prayer and direct evangelization occupied a good part of the day; the aim was to provide for future revivals preachers who would be inspired rather than learned. In 1900 the students broached the subject of baptism of the Spirit; reading the Acts of the Apostles, they were struck by the relationship between the outpouring of the Spirit on the disciples and the speaking in tongues (that is, foreign tongues). They wondered why they themselves did not speak in tongues, and in so doing seemed to discover a lack in the experiences of holiness they had known so far. They shut themselves in their own 'upper room' to pray, and it was there that occurred what was described by one of the participants, Miss Agnes Ozman: 'During the first day of 1901, the Lord was present to us in a remarkable way, calming our hearts and thus enabling them to aspire to the highest things. In the evening the Spirit of prayer was upon us. It was almost eleven o'clock, when I felt the desire to ask if someone would be willing to lay his hands on me in order that I might receive the gift of the Holy Spirit. In the moment when the hands were placed on my head, the Spirit came upon me and I began to speak in tongues, praising God. It was as though streams of living water were welling up from the depths of my being'.[21]

The essence of the Pentecostal movement is present in this brief passage: expectation of an event which transforms and concecates life, and the two practices of baptism in the Spirit with imposition of hands and speaking in tongues. These practices found their propagator in the person of Pastor Charles Parham, director of the school at Topeka (but not involved from the start in the meeting of 1 January 1901). He founded another bible school in Houston, Texas, and there received as one of his students a Black Baptist, William Seymour, who had belonged to the holiness movements. It was the latter who, having settled in Los Angles in 1906, in a house on Azusa Street, popularized the movement and enabled it to expand. In this great Californian city emergent American Pentecostalism was in contact with preachers returning from Europe where they had taken part in a revival in Wales (1904–1906). There, in the course of the evangelization campaigns led by the enthusiasm of the young miner Evan Roberts, there were, as in Topeka, manifestations of glossolalia responding to a prayer for the outpouring of the Spirit. As a result of Azusa Street in America, of the preaching of Pastor Barrat in Norway, and of the Welsh revival, charismatic groups began to spread. They were badly received and discredited in the press. The new Pentecost was reproached for its extravagances, for its link with the Blacks, and for the importance it accorded to the mysterious 'speaking in tongues'. The holiness movements, which had provided it with so many adherents, were not among the last to condemn those from whom they were careful to dissociate themselves. At first, the assemblies based on the Los Angeles model criticised those ecumenical groups whose members had to remain in their respective churches. The hostile attitude of the latter encouraged the charismatics to organize themselves into federations (after 1906) and then into churches. Today there are about two hundred of these throughout the world; the best known are the so-called Assemblies of God. Internal evolutionary factors likewise contributed to this change from a transitory meeting to federated, well-organized group: growth of a press, of institutes of formation, and of a professional ministry, (lay zeal having proved inadequate), the sending of missionaries, the regulation of an enthusiasm which was discovered to be more than merely spiritual.

The Pentecostal movements were well acquainted with controversy and ruptures, some of which are worth recording here because they give some into account the issues involved. Round about 1908, people were wondering whether baptism in the Spirit constituted a third blessing after those of conversion and sanctification (the Los Angeles solution) or whether one should reckon that there are only two blessings (the Chicago solution which retained, of the stages of the spiritual life, a conversion-new birth and a baptism of the Spirit with charismatic manifestations). In 1915 a schism developed around a minority of pastors who were administering baptism in 'the name of Jesus'—a practice supported by a modalist theology and a distrust of baptism in the traditional churches. Debates arose over the question of speaking in tongues—notably in Canada round about 1918—and of the privileged place the groups had accorded it, above the other gifts of the Spirit.[22]

Speaking in Tongues as the Sociological Basis of Pentecostalism

At the end of the debates to which I have just alluded, the conclusion was more obvious than ever for the Pentecostalists: speaking in tongues was the manifestation *par excellence* of baptism in the Spirit. By the same token it was the way of entry into the Pentecostal universe, its rallying sign.

(*a*) From the point of view of our historical sequence, speaking in tongues gave Pentecostalism its specific character. Certainly other Christian groups were familiar among themselves with charismatic practices (including glossolalia)—among nineteenth-century Anglo-Saxons alone there were the Quakers, the followers of E. Irving, and the Adventists. The new element at Topeka and Los Angeles was the indissoluble link made between baptism of the Spirit and speaking in tongues. Now, baptism in the Spirit was the constitutive element of communities of the holiness movement type, to which movement all Pentecostal communities belong. It is not that, within them, baptism in the Spirit is considered absolutely necessary for individual salvation (conversion is sufficient), but it is where one starts from to become fully Christian and prepared for the work of evangelization. Thus speaking in tongues, authenticating the spiritual blessing, serves as a criterion for belonging to the group which unites charismatic practice and the search for holiness. Just as in a revivalist assembly each one asked his neighbour, 'Are you converted?' so the Pentecostalist would always be tempted to ask, 'Do you speak in tongues?' The non-charismatic was not excluded from the prayer meeting, but he quickly understood that he was not really part of it.

Revivalism and the holiness movements, minimizing the role of creed and sacrament, built up the Church on the subjective faith of individuals. One regarded oneself as part of it in the measure that one felt one was converted, sanctified, consecrated. The presence of the Spirit can only be immediately attested through inner conviction, which is not easily communicated; after the event only, spiritual authenticity can be judged by its fruits: fruits of the moral or of the missionary order (for Finney, 'to win an average of five souls to Christ in the course of a year's work' is to 'exhibit signs of alarming weakness!').[22] This completely *a posteriori* verification was all the more subject to varieties of interpretation. With the new Pentecost, the charism, visible concomitant to the spiritual experience, reintroduced objectivity into the criteria for belonging to a religious group. And in a milieu that was tainted with fundamentalism, this objectivity had the merit of being biblical. Of the outward manifestations of spiritual enthusiasm only those consecrated by the experience of the primintive community were retained. But why, one might ask, is speaking in tongues accorded a privileged place among the gifts of the Spirit? The Pentecostalists do not consider speaking in tongues to be more precious than other charisms, such as prophecy and healing; but it is manifest from the start as a minimum always given with baptism of the Spirit.

As Jean Séguy observes, the charism plays a regulating role in the context of spiritual enthusiasm.[23] It introduces into the 'anomic' spontaneity a point of reference exterior to the group; discipline and method are no longer so far removed from pure enthusiasm. In the first place it is a fact that since the tumultuous meetings of Azusa Street (the house, it would seem, trembled on its foundations), the Pentecostalist assemblies became progressively more sober and better organized.

(*b*) The constitutive role of the charism does not imply that it takes the place of conversion or holiness in the Pentecostalist group. There one lived above all in the spirit of the revival. If, in one sense, speaking in tongues regarded holiness as the sign of its own overflowing, it is even more true that holiness regarded speaking in tongues as the goal to be pursued. This much was no doubt understood earlier on from the testimony of Miss Agnes Ozman. A recent manifesto from one of the Pentecostal churches clarifies a number of things: 'It would be a poor baptism of the Spirit that had speaking in tongues as its only sign. Many have been content with that, and they have been mistaken'. The charismatic trend was polarised by the search for holiness. This notion of holiness, inherited from Methodism, and transformed by the missionary needs of American revivalism, is more complex than might appear at first sight: it sometimes takes on a puritanical aspect, but it is also joy and even exuberance. Each one is called upon to employ all his interior energies in acquiring it, but it is, according to the doctrine of justification by faith, essentially a gift received with gratitude. Rather than to a perfectionism focused on the inner life, it encourages total consecration, in order that the work of the Kingdom might be accomplished (the latter being seen in strictly an eschatological light).

In this perspective of holiness through surrender to the Spirit, speaking in tongues is the more readily recognized as a sign in that it reveals itself in practice to signify surrender and encounter with an extraordinary power of jubilation and praise. In the words of Pastor Thomas Brès, it is 'an overflowing of spiritual joy', the 'fervour of adoration'. It is felt to be, not a prodigy, but a gift for the structuring of the Christian life, both of the individual and of the community.[24]

Life of Pentecostalism

Nothing is more liberating, practically and affectively speaking, than involvement in a Pentecostal community. It is very difficult simply to take it or leave it. To take it means, in concrete terms to devote almost all one's free time to the community life of prayer and evangelization. On a Sunday morning in the assemblies of God, prayer lasts on an average two-and-a-half hours. There the 'breaking of bread' is celebrated, the 'Supper', the eschatological significance of which is emphasized. There people make use of their charisms (prophecy), and certain times are set aside for silence; there is less spontaneity than one might have expected: in the beginning, pastors, lay preachers, deacons and deaconesses were designated as such by their charisms, but they strove to channel quite as much as to quicken the charism of others. After a meal, which was frequently taken in common, the afternoon was given over to evangelization in some neutral spot (sometimes outside). All sang, had the chance to bear witness, prayed for the cure of the sick, and were urged to become converted, conversion being concretely signified by genuflection at the proclamation of penitents in certain Pentecostalist churches (as also in the Salvation Army). On weekday evenings various meetings brought the charismatics together: assemblies for prayer, bible school, societies for women or young people, and so on.

Pentecostalism is a response to the need for a simple religion, not highly conceptualized and rich in events. Those who are allergic to it will easily see in it a fine conditioning process. Those who are won over to it will speak, on the other hand, of a place of liberating encounter. The historian need not decide between them; he has learnt not to be surprised that what is alienation for some is freedom for others, and vice versa. At all events, the social success of Pentecostalism shows that it responds well both to the aspirations and to the faults of our society.

Pentecostalism and Society

Pentecostalism expanded vigorously in the United States (at the beginning of the century the figure for growth was given as 10.7 per cent annually, as against 6 or 8 per cent in the other confessions). It was particularly successful among the Blacks, the Puerto Ricans, the rootless peasants in the towns, and artisans threatened by the crisis.[25] It is possible, however, to define it as a confession corresponding to a particular social milieu; as it evolved it spread more among the cultivated sectors of the population, or else through the discipline it imposed, favoured, a certain degree of social advancement for its members. But a sociological study of Pentecostalism is interested in showing that it provides for many misfits in industrial society with a channel through which to express their bewilderment, and at the same time to discover some kind of spiritual home. 'Pentecostal teaching', writes Bryan Wilson, 'allows for the expression of intense feelings which would otherwise, no doubt, have been suppressed . . . Other sects might have assured their members of a life in common, but Pentecostalism was alone in truly responding, through its expressive force, to the conditions in which many Americans were living . . . thus becoming the most complete manifestation of a faith which authorised and even sanctified the expression of the strongest emotions'.[26]

In more precise terms, this response to a life situation was the response to its life situation of a minority passing through an identity crisis or cut off from its roots. There is, therefore, nothing surprising in the fact that Pentecostalism, the religion of this minority, and one which had a strong hold on life as a whole, could be interpreted as an element of 'counter-culture'. It rejected a number of the values on which American society was based, and proved that one could be happy doing without them. Thus the puritanism of the charismatics was characterized by rejection, in some measure, of consumption (rejection, that is, more or less urgently encouraged according to the different groups, of alcohol, tobacco, the cinema, television and elegance in the matter of dress. This Pentecostal abstinence was not obedience to an ascetical discipline based on a value system or to a spiritualist philosophy; it referred continually to an eschatological horizon, to the desire to announce that 'this world is passing away' and that we live with other riches than those we find here. It undoubtedly constituted an element of protest against the comfort on which American society was based. However, it is not difficult to see that this protest did not lead to revolution, and the marginalization it created could only serve to reassure the 'haves'. What is more, Pentecostalism tended to attack luxury rather than 'dishonest' wealth; it was relatively short-sighted when it came to grasping the social implications of the evangelism which it awakened in the individual convert (some communities, for example, which were very quick to warn their adherents of the harmfulness of tobacco had nothing to say to them about the war in Vietnam).

Although it was not an immediate threat to the dominant culture, Puritanism in the Pentecostal perspective was an element of counterculture. So too was mistrust of critical theology. The new Pentecost appeared at a time when Modernism was penetrating the teaching of the American Protestant churches with the influence of the 'Hegelian Left' in the universities and the desire to eliminate the "supernatural" from all discussion of faith. A more 'liberal' Christianity was being spread abroad, a Christianity more adapted to the ideas of a world that was proud of its progress. It was gaining acceptance among the growing number of those who had been favoured by economic progress and who were happy to be able to establish a link between their religious faith and the science which was the fundamental element of a world in progress. But what Christianity gained in the ability to adapt, did it not lose in the strength of its free and complete affirmation of itself?—which is where Pentecostalism came in, with its uncompromising fundamentalism (the Bible, with no concessions), its practical belief in miracles and its feeling for a God who intervenes, upsetting the order of things. The misfits, the Blacks, all those for whom the progress was not progress, had few reasons for rejoicing at the harmony of liberal theology; they had more cause to wonder at the charisms through which the Word was given to the uncultured and 'Power from on High' to those without power. Paradoxically, moreover, Pentecostalist teaching, which had very little that was scientific or modernist (or conformist) about it, corresponded to certain contemporary aspirations: that of seeking the truth in lived experience, of finding its immediate verification in the moral life of the community; that of not accepting God unless one could go to him with the whole of oneself.

In season and out of season, from the beginning of this century, Pentecostalism has been denouncing the faults of the consumer society and the inadequacy of one single language—the language of science—in enabling man to discover his own truth. On this point its partisans and its adversaries are in agreement, though they disagree about the quality of the response brought by these mysterious charisms.

THIRD STAGE: CATHOLIC NEO-PENTECOSTALISM SINCE 1967

Misunderstood by the churches, but strong in its own experience, Pentecostalism, before World War II, presented itself as a movement, formed of divers groups and largely closed to the outside—it was a stranger, for example, to the ecumenical movement. This attitude was not definitive. For several decades now we have been witnessing the spread of charismatic practices to all sorts of Christian communities. In 1932, for example, a Welsh evangelist led a revival in the parishes of the French Reformed Church in Ardèche, during which he urged the 'converted' to remain within their own denominations. In other cases, groups would adopt charismatic practices without seeking, in so doing, to constitute an assembly of Pentecostal churches. In 1945, and again in 1957, in the United States, the use of charisms became widespread among Episcopalians and Christians of the most 'respectable' confessions, whose traditions implied mistrust of all enthusiasm. This was neo-Pentecostalism.[27] In this way, charismatic practices came to appear less and less closely linked with milieux that were too clearly defined sociologically or historically; increasingly they came to be regarded as efficacious in the context of the renewal of Christian life as a whole. In 1966, the current reached some Catholic groups: at that time, some young students at Duquesne University in Pittsburgh, conscious of the inadequacies of an over-cerebral Christianity, and longing for a new inspiration in order to implement the *aggiornamento* called for by Pope John XXIII, fasted, invoked the Holy Spirit and read Pentecostalist literature (*The Cross and the Switchblade* by Wilkerson and J. Sherill's *They Speak in Other Tongues*).[28] Then, in January 1967, they came into contact with the neo-Pentecostalist members of a prayer assembly of the Episcopal Church. Several of them received the baptism of the Spirit and, in February, weekend meetings were held, in the course of which the charismatic experience was lived through for the first time by a typically Catholic group who aimed through it to strengthen their attachment to the Church. One witness was to describe it as 'a striking example of the swift and merciful action of the Holy Spirit towards those who open themselves to him'.[29]

The rapid spread of neo-Pentecostalism in the United States and then, after 1970, to all continents, its prayer groups its communities (parishes as in Providence, 'households' in Ann Arbor), and its great meetings are all sufficiently familiar, particularly to readers of *Concilium,* for me not to have to discuss them further here.[30]

From Pentecostalism to Neo-Pentecostalism

It should not cause surprise that there are manifest differences between Pentecostalism and neo-Pentecostalism, especially Catholic neo-Pentecostalism.[31] A charismatic group, almost by definition, is little concerned with adopting a particular style or respecting a tradition. The Catholic groups are in general more concerned to integrate themselves into the movement of their Church than to be in line with the experiences of Topeka and Los Angeles (the existence of which many are unaware).

Between Pentecostalism and neo-Pentecostalism the sociological impact has shifted. The original group in Pittsburgh was a group of students; subsequently the trend did not appear to be attached to any particular milieu; if one compares this, however, with the beginnings at Los Angeles, the predominance of misfits and cuturally deprived has completely disappeared (which does not rule out the very real attraction of the marginalised towards the charismatic movements). Charismaticism has very little doctrine about it. This makes it easier of access to practising Catholics who believe they have nothing to subtract from or add to their fundamental *credo.* A practice, however, is never neutral. That involving the gifts in Pentecostalism points to a revival of the meaning of grace as gartuitousness and as the transforming principle in man; it gives the impression of bridging the gap that separates us from the Bible, from the distant past which it recalls as promises for the future, whence the acceptance of a less critical faith, and sometimes even of a certain fundamentalism; the charismative movement in contemporary Catholicism is as opposed to a return to formalistic conservatism (spontaneity must be free) as it is to the modernistic reduction of faith to nothing more than an interpretation of human experience.

The prayer assemblies, communities of sharing and meetings during holiday periods are times for deepening biblical knowledge and for reflexion on charismatic practice. In this way the beginnings of a Catholic theology of charismatic practices was elaborated. One of its great concerns has been to show that 'baptism in the Holy Spirit' does not interfere with the fulness of sacramental baptism. 'Baptism of the Spirit', writes Ranaghan, 'does not replace baptism and confirmation. Rather, it comes as an adult reaffirmation and renewal of these sacraments, an opening of ourselves to all the graces they bring'.[32] In order to avoid all confusion and any suspicion that the sacramental rites are insufficient, the expression 'baptism of the Spirit' is usually replaced among Catholics by that of 'outpouring of the Spirit'. The history of the holiness movements permits us to place 'baptism in the Spirit' in the line which runs from a first conversion to a second 'blessing' or 'consecration'. Catholics were unfamiliar with this; their prayer 'for the outpouring' is a simple *epiclesis* to which one awaits an answer, while the person over whom one is praying becomes further engaged in the way of conversion. However, there is now a tendency towards greater strictness, towards more control of the demand for this prayer, without there being any reference made, however, to the Pentecostalist doctrine of the two or three 'blessings'.

The Catholic reinterpretation thus gives relative importance to 'baptism in the Spirit', at the same time allowing it to be a powerful experience (those who do not agree with the practice would say psychologically powerful). The charisms too are given relative importance, in the sense that no one of them emerges as necessarily accompanying the fulness of the gift and entry into the community of true Christians. People are more concerned to integrate the use of speaking in tongues, prophecy and healing into a spiritual process which is already known to tradition in outline.

Since the individual aims to live within the Church, the charismatic group is not organized in such a way as to govern the entire Christian and human existence of its members. The few functions exercised at meetings or in communities are not a substitute for the Catholic ministry; the moral directives are no different from those received in the Catholic community in which one is already living (except in cases where there is community of life). Attendance at meetings is more or less regular. Catholic Pentecostalism is less disciplined than the original Pentecostalism, and it leaves more room for lay initiative. Not being itself a church and existing within a structured church, it can allow itself far greater flexibility.

The Hour of Neo-Pentecostalism

Neo-Pentecostalism cannot be explained sociologically simply as a continuation of Pentecostalism. It is not the reaction of misfits or those who are culturally deprived. Counter-cultural elements nevertheless remain within it. If it does not inspire a systematic attitude of puritanical abstinence and flight from the world, it opens up the way to an evangelical radicalism that is more inclined to stress the points of difference than to adapt to 'the world'. Science and the introduction of some degree of criticism into discussion of the faith (notably where exegesis is concerned) are not rejected as diabolical; but one does not want to be afraid of bearing open witness to miracles, to the identifiable intervention of God and to the growth of the new Christian reality which surpasses all expectations. In the conduct of his practical as of his mystical life, the charismatic is someone who will be little understood by those who are too much in the grips of the ideology of science and progress.

Perhaps enough has now been said to explain the passage from popular Pentecostalism to a less socially biassed neo-Pentecostalism. At the beginning of this century, especially in the United States, it was difficult to escape from the influence of science, consumption and liberal optimism, unless one was on the sidelines of material and cultural progress. Today the situation has been reversed. Consumption and science are in a fairly healthy state and lie behind much that goes on; but they no longer have any prestige. Cultural values need to be redefined, and Pentecostalism is, in one sense, one of the counter-cultures that is coming forward to make this redefinition. Consumption alienates, and science gives but a partial knowledge.

The churches are finding it very difficult to discover a language that will awaken interest in the things of faith. Discourse carried out on the traditional lines is no longer understood by the majority of our contemporaries. That which attempts to integrate the language of the new critical and scientific rationalisms is scarcely more successful: it is too technical, it smacks of compromise, and its neutrality leaves one cold. Why should one be detached if one has never been involved? The charismatic experience, which has something more to offer besides its language, has a chance. It speaks of the essentials of faith, of Jesus and of the Gospel as if they were there. No doubt the charismatic must learn also that they are not there yet and must always be sought after. The Church will offer him its powers of intercession, its tradition and its sacraments. His faith will only survive through the effort to achieve some degree of integration into his cultural world (which is not done without compromise). But will he not do even that, because the charismatic experience will have given him the desire and the courage to grasp the object of faith, which always escapes us? Some people will think me optimistic, considering that what they call the charismatic illusion paralyzes all research. But at least there will be agreement as to the fact that there is a coincidence between the growth of neo-Pentecostalism and the crisis of language in our world and in the Church.

So the spread of neo-Pentecostalism can be seen as a sign (among many others of course) that men and women of all walks of life have become what the depressed classes were during an American crisis at the beginning of this century—bewildered, deprived beings, and for that reason (one must believe) in a certain sense more human. But to point up the faults of our society, and the functional difficulties of the Church which correspond to them is not to say much about such tendencies as the charismatic movements. Were one to leave the matter there, one would lay oneself open to understanding them as reactions or refuges, and it would be dangerously easy to prove that they are indeed reactions and refuges. Now they see themselves as dynamic rather than repressive, exultant rather than mournful, and as bearing witness rather then protesting. The revivalists of the age of the camp meeting told us that they reflected the situation of the frontier with its possibilities for expansion. Something of this reflection has remained, although Pentecostalism has left the frontier. The Church that is now there to be built up is the Church of *aggiornamento* and *oikoumene;* the Spirit invoked there is, in God, not cold immateriality but the breath of life, he who 'hastens the time', who pushes back the limits of the possible and shares his joy.

Translated by Sarah Fawcett

Notes

1. It is easy enough to relate religious movements to socio-economic or cultural facts; it is a much more difficult and risky matter to discern what is mere coincidence, what the preparation of favourable ground, and what is a determining factor. On the other hand, the explanations of sociologists are soon too narrow or too general to be convincing. Hence, to take the example of neo-Pentecostalism, it spread to Canada during a year which saw a failure of the 'Québéquois' party (1970). The juxtaposition of these facts lends itself to ingenious considerations: the failure created a gap which people filled with new affective goals. But who would dare to assert that in the event of a Québéquois victory the 'charismatics' would only have elicited a small response? On the contrary, to speak of the instability of life in society as a factor in spiritual upheavals does not amount to very much, since it is possible to detect elements of social instability in most ages and milieux. That which explains much explains nothing, and one should no doubt look for a middle way between this too much and the too little. I do not feel that the sociologists have found it as far as 'charismaticism' is concerned.

2. Testimony of Finney, cited by G. Swarts, *Salut par la foi et conversion brusque* (Paris, 1931), p. 276–7.

3. Cf. Dickson D. Bruce, *And they all sang Hallelujah: Plain-Folk Camp-meeting Religion (1800–1845)* (Knoxville, 1974). On American Methodism cf. William W. Sweet, *Religion on the American Frontier* (Chicago, 1946).

4. I use the word here in the non-pejorative sense of groups of Christians, united by their acceptance of particular revelations. The Adventists are 'sectarian', whereas the Pentecostalists are not.

5. B. Wilson, *Les Sectes Religiouses* (Paris, 1970), p. 65.

6. Cf. Finney's dissertation on religious revivals (Geneva-Vevey, 1886), p. 319.

7. *Op. cit.*, p. 162. This comparison with Catholic doctrine does not imply any particular affinity in Finney with regard to Catholicism.

8. The language of 'revival' assumes that the listener believes that God exists, that he speaks through the Bible, and that he demands a life that is pious, sober and dedicated to others. The effort consists in making a man pass from dormant knowledge to resolution, and in suggesting that the hour of grace has come. In spite of American pragmatism, the sense of divine intervention remains more marked in these Protestant discourses than in those of the Catholic 'missions'.

9. The Methodists were among the most active supporters of the abolition of slavery. Dissatisfied with the compromises of their Church (MEC), they formed anti-slavery conventions, which provoked a schism. Finney too is resolutley abolitionist: he regarded the churches' timidity in opposing the institution of slavery in the southern states as one of the things which prevented them from profiting from 'revivals'. However, revivalism and Methodism are more concerned with private morality than with socio-political problems.

10. If the Catholic mystics have frequently exalted non-affectivity, they have also relied on affectivity, source for them of an inner persuasion which they share with us unaffectedly, cf. Pascal's *Mémorial;* St Ignatius' description of the interior graces he received at Manresa, which were such that, were the scriptures to disappear, they would sustain his faith; and St Teresa of Avila's *Interior Castle,* 'Fifth Mansion', ch. 1.

11. Finney, *op. cit.,* p. 11.

12. *Op. cit.,* p. 1. This use of sensibility in the interest of the rational choice of lived faith aligns Finney with the Catholic missionaries of the Counter-Reformation and explains the opposition he encountered in Presbyterian circles. It should be noted that there is nowhere to be found in him an exaltation of affectivity as being, of itself, more religious than reason.

13. Cf. Luther, *On Christian Liberty,* no. 10.

14. Wesley did not think, however, that a 'saint' could achieve impeccability. Cf. H. Lindstrom, *Wesley and Sanctification* (London, no date).

15. Cf. Charles G. Finney, *Etre revétu de la puissance d'En Haut* (Geneva, 1886), pp. 10, 11, 15, 16.

16. Quoted in J. Séguy, *Les Sectes Protestantes dans la France contemporaine* (Paris, 1956), p. 256.

17. It would have more links with the practice of confirmation in the Orthodox and Catholic Churches, but retained none of the appearance of a sacrament.

18. At the end of his discourse on 'reclothing', *op. cit.,* p. 19, Finney admits that one can be consecrated to the Holy Spirit without being aware of it at the moment it happens.

19.   Modalism is the doctrinal tendency which takes the three names of the Trinity to be no more than aspects of a single divine person. For modalism in the revivalist movements, cf. Hollenweger, p. 30 (see below).

20. On Pentecostalism cf. Nils Bloch-Holl, *The Pentecostal Movement* (London, 1964); Hollenweger, *Enthusiastisches Christentum: die Pfingst-Bewegung* (Zürich, 1969); Jean Séguy, 'Situation historique du Pentecôtisme' in *Lumière et Vie* no. 125 (November 1975); and so on. I have greatly relied on notes taken during a session on the 'charismatic movements' at the Centre Thomas More (Eveux sur l'Arbresle), at which the instructor was J. Séguy.

21.   Cited in Séguy, *op. cit.,* p. 35.

22.   Cf. Hollenweger, *op. cit.,* p. 25–62.

23.   *Lumière et Vie* no. 125, p. 46.

24.   *The Assembly of the Living God,* 'Ta Volonté' (Moyen, no date), p. 17.

25.   Séguy places the expansion of Pentecostalism in the context of the agricultural crisis of the Middle West and the disappointments that followed the Civil War. According to a survey carried out in 1936, the results of which are quoted in Bloch Hoell (p. 57) and Hollenweger (p. 27), the proportion of Blacks in the Pentecostal movement was 14.5 per cent, as against 9.7 per cent in the United States population as a whole. The average income of the Pentecostalist was $735, compared with an average of $2749 for the population as a whole. It was therefore a confession for people of lower status.

26.   B. Wilson, *op. cit.,* p. 72.

27.   On this Protestant neo-Pentecostalism, see Hollenweger, *op. cit.,* ch. 1; B. Wilson, *op. cit.;* A. E. Bremond, *Sur le cemin du renouveau,* (Paris, 1976).

28.   David Wilkerson, *The Cross and the Switchblade;* John H. Scherill, *Ils parlent d'autres langues* (Jura, 1969).

29.   K. and D. Ranaghan, *The Return of the Spirit.*

30.   With the books mentioned in notes 28 and 29, compare Ed O'Connor, *The Charismatic Renewal: Origins and Perspectives;* René Laurentin, *Pentecôtisme chez les Catholiques. Risques et avenir* (Paris, 1974); Cardinal Suenens, *A New Pentecost?* (London, 1974); L. Boisset *Mouvement de Jésus et Renouveau dans l'Esprit,* (CTM de Meylan, 1974); John Randall, *Providence, Birth of a Catholic Charismatic Parish;* Pierre Gallay, *Croyants hors frontières* (Paris, 1975). Cf. *Concilium,* nos. 89, pp. 91–9 and 79, 83–7, etc.

31.   Catholic neo-Pentecostalism and Protestant neo-Pentecostalism practise a large measure of ecumenism among themselves—some groups are completely mixed; others are open to those of the other confession.

32.   Cf. Ranaghan, *op. cit.,* p. 28.

Enrique Dussel

The Differentiation of Charisms

THE numerous works dealing with charisms[1] show a considerable weakness, if not a total lack, of principle by which to guide the typological division of charisms. They generally try to elaborate a more or less coherent typology from the New Testament, forgetting that this deals with the Church at the moment of its foundation only. On the other hand, institutional and clerical ecclesiology has—with a certain guilt complex—been at pains to demonstrate the "accidental" connection between charism and the hierarchical ministry or institution, omitting to explain the necessary definition of charism inside the structure of the Church (prophetic-institutional) as opposition, 'contradiction', conflict within the one community called to *last* in history (institution) in order to *innovate* and criticize history (charism), and finally to die: there will be neither ecclesial institution nor charisms in the Kingdom.

SOME TYPOLOGIES OF CHARISM

The *Practices of the Apostles* (the true translation of *Praxeis Apostolōn*) gives no typology, but only accounts of charismatic practices. The founding of the Church is a charismatic experience: 'When the day of Pentecost came round, they were all together in the same room and there suddenly came a sound from heaven . . . (and) they were all filled with the Holy Spirit and began to speak in strange tongues' (*Acts* 2:1–4.). In the same way, Peter healed the sick (3:1–11), the faithful carried out acts of service to each other with 'singular graces' (*charis megalē*) (4:32–37), helping at table (6:1–7), giving witness of their teaching in their lives (7:1–60), and so on. Taking all these charismatic practices together, it should be possible, as Belo has shown, to construct a typology of this NT narrative.

Paul, for his part, provides the basic materials for all future typologies. It is as well to list them here, abbreviated, so that we can number them for later use:

1 Cor. 12:8–10		*1 Cor. 12:28–30*		*Rom. 12:6–8*		*Eph. 4:11*	
1.1	*logos sophias*	2.1	Apostle	3.1	Prophet	4.1	Apostle
1.2	*logos gnōseōs*	2.2	Prophet	3.2	Deacons	4.2	Prophet
1.3	Faith	2.3	Master	3.3	Master	4.3	Evangelist
1.4	Healing	2.4	Miracles	3.4	Exhortation	4.4	Pastor
1.5	Miracles	2.5	Healing	3.5	Alms	4.5	Master
1.6	Prophecy	2.6	Helping	3.6	President		
1.7	Discernment	2.7	Ruling	3.7	Works of		
1.8	Tongues	2.8	Tongues		mercy		
1.9	Interpretation of tongues						

Later theology built its typologies on the basis of these lists. To take three examples: For St Thomas Aquinas, *I-II*, q. 111, a. 4, resp., charisms are *gratia gratis data*,[2] and, following the list in 1 Cor. 12:8–10, ordered to 'the other', i.e., 'teaching and persuading externally only, since only God can move internally'. They can be divided as in the table below.

Gratia gratis data for the instruction of our neighbour in the things of the faith	1. For perfect knowledge	*Faith* or special certainty about principles (1.3) *Sermo sapientiae* or on the principal conclusions of science (1.1) *Sermo scientiae* or on the examples or effects of causes (1.2)	
	2. As confirmation of revelation	Through works Through knowledge	*Gratia sanitatum* (1.4) *Operatio virtutum* (1.5) *Prophetia* (1.6) *Discretio spiritum* (1.7)
	3. Help in preaching the word	*Genera linguarum* (1.8) *Interpretatio sermonum* (1.9)	

St Thomas sees the principle of the difference between charisms as residing in the fact that they serve 'to instruct others in divine matters' (*ad hoc quod alterum instruat in rebus divinis*). It should be borne in mind that 'instruction' has to do only with theory (except for 1.4 and 1.5), with the intellectual or teaching level.

Completing and correcting this typology, H. Leclerq[3] divides charisms into: (i) those relating to the instruction of the faithful (1.6, 2.1, 2.3, 4.3, 3.4, 1.3, 1.7, 1.8, 1.9 and similar); (ii) those relating to corporal works (2.6, 3.2, 3.5, 1.4, 1.5 and similar); (iii) those relating to government (4.4, 3.6, 2.7). It is interesting to note his view that: 'charisms, a precious stimulant to maintaining the fervour of small communities, become impracticable and disturbing (sic) as the definitive organization of the Church becomes established'.[4] This is an indication of the accidental value accorded to charisms in Catholic ecclesiology till the last few decades.

Küng proposes a very similar typology: (i) charisms of preaching; (ii) charisms of help; (iii) charisms of guidance or direction; he does, however, add some categories to the list, such as 'counsellors' (par. 1), deaconesses, widows who care for the sick (par. 2), bishops (par. 3), and: 'all these do not exhaust the variety of charisms . . . Suffering too should be counted as a charism (cf. 1 Cor. 1:24). Basically, all *vocation* is a *participation* (cf. 1 Cor. 7:17) in *charism* (cf. Rom. 12:3, 6)'.[5]

The second Vatican Council returned to the established typology of charisms; 'the extraordinary ones (*clarissima*) and the simple and common ones (*simpliciora et latius diffusa*) . . . should both be received with gratitude and comfort . . . But judgment (*iudicium*) on their authenticity (*genuinitate*) and application belongs to those who hold authority in the Church'.[6]

Since 1970 there has been talk of a new division of charisms: some would belong to the self-styled 'charismatic movements'; others to those who commit themselves in the political sphere. Between the two there is real confrontation and contradiction, and dialogue is often impossible. Perhaps 'these contradictions are a sign of the vitality of a Church renewing itself in turmoil'?[7]

THE NEED FOR A THEORETICAL FRAMEWORK

Our task is to define the principle that guides the differentiation between charisms. What follows is an attempt, and only an attempt, to open discussion on a theme that has considerable contemporary relevance.

2.1 Charisms and Functional Sociology

Max Weber, for example, opposes charism to the bureaucratic or patriarchal exercise of authority.[8] The objective rationality of the bureaucratic approach and traditional structure of authority tend to lend permanence to the established order. The charismatic, on the other hand, possesses creative power and freedom, and launches out on a crusade to change the social order. Charisms can have either a political or a religious bent. The charismatic authority, the natural leader, possesses extraordinary physical and spiritual gifts: he is the hero. His political power and legitimacy inspire loyalty, fidelity and faith. The prophet, the religious charismatic like Zoroaster, Jesus or Mahommed, is the bringer of salvation (*Heilbringer*), who opposes the established order. Weber goes on to analyze the question in pre-capitalism, and in modern capitalism, seeing charism in relation to the question of stratification, status, social class. He makes several notable points.

Talcott Parsons, to take another example, shows that every social system produces a crystallization of its structure through differentiated determination of different roles. Two situations are the exceptions to this rule: that of deviant[9] or pathological behaviour (that of the thief, for example), and social change,[10] which brings a 'charismatic revolutionary movement'—such as Nazism saw itself, for example. Parsons holds that change can be effected *within* a system (through change of a sub-system), but that there can be no change *of* the system in its totality. The first type of change operating against the dominant system is through illegal action, crime; the second is through irrational behaviour, exceptional by definition. This theoretical framework leaves charism ill-defined, since, as we shall see, it operates on the level of innovatory capacity, of historical change, as a real *virtus liberationis* (taking *virtus* in its sense of *vir,* not of 'virtue').

2.2   Charisms, Means of Production and Processes

The function of the Church in history is, precisely, to stand up against social systems structured by domination or sin, or historical entities characterized by these, in order to set them on a new course of becoming more perfect systems so as to prepare for the Coming of the Lord in his Parousia. Charism, as we shall see, is precisely a dialectical force of re-direction, of de-structuration of the unjust entity. So we need categories or theoretical frameworks that will allow us to understand the problem of passing from one system to another: of social change.

'Means of production', for example, is an abstract category or concept designating an economic, political or ideological entity, an entity self-produced by man and which conditions his existence. The Pauline charisms were enumerated in a society whose means of production was based partly on tribute and partly on slavery (the Hellenic province of the Roman empire, which can be taken as the 'social structure' of the time, its particular historical entity). It is important to realize[11] that transition from the predominance of one means of production to predominance of another within the same social structure, is produced mainly by development of the productive forces, by technological progress—as Darcy Ribeiro, among others, has shown.

So, for example, St Benedict's *ora et labora,* in the fifth century, can be seen as a charismatic collaboration with the growing productive force of the barbarians within the Empire, who, by replacing slave labour, installed a new society based on the productive force of the serf in the feudalism that was to follow. The transition or social change from Roman slave-based society to feudal Europe, or to modern capitalism, was not achieved without struggle and conflict, nor without dismantling means of production and modifying the articulation of economic, political and ideological processes. The Benedictines, who had been charismatic communities at the outset of pre-feudalism, did not act in the same way as the Mendicants in the crisis of medieval society, when pre-mercantile capitalist means of production were beginning to appear in the cities of central Italy, southern France and the Spain of the Reconquest.

One can then understand how the 'institutional' Church tends, through being structured to give itself permanence, to bless the means of production and the articulation of processes hallowed by time, once they have become established by long secular custom. St Thomas himself admitted the *iustum dominativum*[12] of the feudal lord over his serfs, thereby giving his blessing to the medieval system of tribute.

We need to appreciate, however, that charisms do not only operate on a theoretical or ideological supra-structural level, but that they can mobilize praxis, historical action, the productive forces of the Christian, religious (or even pagan) people. Charism belongs to the infrastructure: the Spirit inspires the growth of productive forces—those that upset the existing means of production and re-launch social structures on successive stages towards the parousia.

The mere suggestion of this line of approach is enough to show the distance that separates a Talcott Parsons or a Max Weber from theologians, whose categories are totally inadequate for an understanding of the question as it is often posed on the periphery—in Latin America.

2.3   Charisms and Social Classes

In the same way, as each means of production is determined by at least two main opposed classes (the lord and the serf in the medieval tribute system, for example), and as each social structure usually contains more than one means of production (although one will be the dominant one), there will be a variety of social classes, stratified in relation to the exercise of economic, political and ideological power at any given moment of social evolution.

So the Church, enshrined as it is in a social fabric, cannot avoid (particularly since the fourth century) having members from many different social classes, inevitably in conflict with each other by reason of their economic, political or ideological status. Since Constantine, at least in Byzantine, Western and Latin-American Christendoms, the hierarchy of the ecclesial institution came to act in some capacity within the social structure, seen at least as a *locus* for the exercise of ideological power; and in medieval Christendom and that of colonial Latin America, for the exercise of economic and political power as well. One can then understand how the mere fact of being a bishop or priest in these Christendoms placed one in the dominant social classes of the corresponding social order. So, if charisms are a call from the Spirit to innovate change in history, there is an inevitable social and ecclesial conflict between ministry and charism.

This is said to show that the problem is a tough one, and that theology needs to introduce a closer reference to modern critical social sciences.

2.4   Charisms and an 'Actantial' Model

The works of Vladimir Propp[13] and Algirdas Greimas[14] (who coined the term *actantial*) have shown that popular Christian religiosity plays an active role in worship (arrow *a* in Fig. 1) and a passive one in receiving the desired object (arrow *b*). The mediator (M), the saint who is asked for a miracle or favour (O: a good harvest, a safe journey, good

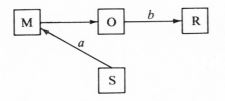

S: subject, or people
M: mediator, or hero
O: object
R: recipient
R=S

Fig. 1

health), is always one who hands the object over to one who asks and receives passively (R). This passivity of the people is often cultivated by a wrong-headed, traditional and fetishistic form of ministry. Charism, on the other hand (see Fig. 2), serves to mobilize the subject (S), to give him strength to cultivate, produce and help himself to the object (O):

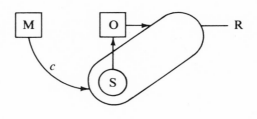

Fig. 2

The people then become protagonists of the history of salvation (arrow *c*); they become the hero or prophet—Moses leaving the desert and leading the people into the Promised Land (O). The *gratia gratis data* was intended to demonstrate just the service rendered by the prophet (S) to the whole people (R).

These simple illustrations do not claim to exhaust the subject: merely to show the need for a more adequate theoretical framework.

CHARISMATIC CALLING AND PRAXIS

A particular example will serve to clarify a doctrinal position. In his *Testament* of 1564, Bartolomé de las Casas recalls the day of his conversion: it was in 1514, and followed his reading of some verses from Ecclesiasticus 34: 'In his goodness and mercy, God saw fit to *choose me,* unworthy as I was, for his ministry, in order to gain the people we call Indians in those parts . . . so as to give them back their original freedom and to liberate them from the violent death they still suffer'.[15]

The minister Bartolomé, a priest exercising the grace of his institutional ministry, before saying mass that day, had read: 'Like one who sacrifices a son (the Indian) before the eyes of his father (God), like one who offers the goods of the poor in sacrifice' (Eccl. 34.20). The bread he was offering was the fruit of the *entrusted* Indians (those who paid a savage tribute to the priest Bartolomé in Cuba). The minister received his grace, charism, through the goodness and mercy of God, 'unworthy as he was', like an election, a calling to perform a task, a labour (Hebrew *habodáh*), a new service that his ministry as such did not require of him. The labour this charism inspired and forced him to was a *political* work (to give the Indians back the freedom they had enjoyed before the coming of the *conquistadores*), an *economic* one ('to liberate them from the violent death they still suffer . . . thefts, murders and usurpations of the estates and tenures of their natural kings and chiefs, of lands and kingdoms and an infinity of other goods'), and an ideological one: 'out of compassion at seeing so many perish . . . when they should have been embraced by our holy Catholic faith . . .'.[16]

His charismatic practice had a critical side to it: *negation of the negation* of 'the other': 'I hold as certain and firmly believe . . . that everything committed by the Spaniards against those people, all their thefts, murders and usurpations . . . has been contrary to the most righteous and immaculate law of Jesus Christ, and contrary to all natural reason'.[17] But it also had a constructive side: 'I have laboured at the court of the kings of Castille, coming and going from the Indies to Castille, and from Castille to the Indies, many times in the course of some fifty years, since 1514'.[18]

The charism he received was then a calling or vocation from the Spirit promoting historical innovation in terms of criticism of the ruling system and the building of a new order on the political, economic and ideological levels for the members of the ecclesial community, in the 'Church→World', 'Church→Church' and 'World→World' relationships, as we shall see.

It is worth remembering that Bartolomé heard his call through discovering the relationship between the 'matter' of his sacrifice—the bread—and the 'historical injustice' by which he received the bread—the tributary system of production known as the *encomienda*. His charism fulfilled the essential moment of religion ('I want mercy and not sacrifices'): the production and distribution of 'bread' in justice: that is, the mobilization of history towards the parousia. Charism offers worship throughout history, just as ministry celebrates the history of liberation in liturgy.

TOWARDS A TYPOLOGY OF CHARISMS

It is possible, at least hypothetically, to divide the infinite variety of charisms—varying with person, class, age, function—into a certain typology that will allow us to classify the present practices of the Church. If the object of charisms is 'the perfecting of the saints in the tasks that befall them' (*eis ergon diakonias*, Eph. 4:11), we should try to classify charisms in terms of these 'tasks' (*ergon*). A charism is defined by its function.

In *Lumen Gentium,* n. 12, we read: 'the people of God shares in the *prophetic* gift of Christ'. It would seem in fact that the central charism, to which all others are related, is the charism of prophecy (found in the four lists from St Paul: 1.6, 2.2, 3.1, and 4.2), and I shall construct the typology accordingly.

The following diagram (Fig. 3) sums up what has been said so far and gives a graphic explanation of what follows:

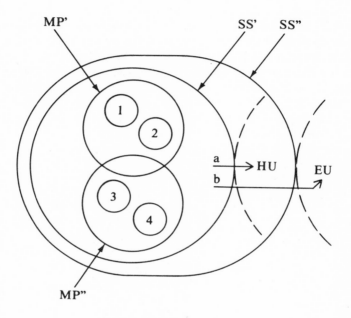

Fig. 3

The Church, and therefore the charismatic calling, exists within a particular social structure (SS') (different in, e.g., the United States, Mexico and Cuba). Therefore the Church undergoes the contradictions inherent in the social structure, those produced by different means of production (MP' in Mexico, for example, would be capitalist, and MP" traditional or semi-tributary) and the social classes that go with them (the diagram gives: 1. bourgeoisie, 2. industrial workers, 3. land-owning peasants, 4. serfs, communal farm workers, indigenous communities, etc.). Charisms emerge in all structural situations, and take account of the fact that the means of production have different applications: political, economic and ideological. In a situation of change, there is a tendency (arrow *a*) towards an historical Utopia (HU), and in the case of the Church the process is re-directed towards an eschatological Utopia (EU), the specific function of charism.

Let us now examine the different components of the matter.

4.1   Charisms in the Prophetic "Church→Social Structure" Sphere

The 'task' of the Church is the conversion, liberation and salvation of the world, of history. The Church is justified through its saving action. So let us start with this. It is a process of historical-eschatological praxis. The Spirit promotes, within the Church but also outside it (cf. 4.1.3 and 4.3), the innovative capabilities needed to free the world from sin and so save it.

4.1.1   Kerygmatic-Ideological Critical Charisms

The Spirit primarily promotes criticism of the social structure and its means of production, operating as negation of negation, on the level where the system looks for its ideological justification. In order to effect his criticism, the charismatic must clearly operate from the hermeneutical standpoint of the oppressed classes (cf. 2.3), as an 'organic intellectual' of the process of liberation. So a Bartolomé challenges the ruling system by proclaiming: 'God must pour down his fury and wrath on Spain, because the whole of Spain has, to a greater or lesser degree, participated in the bloody riches stolen and evilly usurped and badly come by . . . And till now it has not seen that such scandal and infamy . . . has been sin and the greatest injustice'.[19] The prophet criticizes, clarifies the meaning and stirs the foundations of the ideology that cloaks domination; he de-fetishizes the system; he declared himself atheist before its idols.

The charism of tongues and their interpretation (1.8 and 1.9) fall into this category, as do that of the Master (2.3 and 3.3), and Exhortation (3.4), but *ad extra,* as in the preaching of Peter (Acts 2:4 ff). Criticism is brought to bear on the social structure (SS') from the historical Utopia (in Cuba in 1959, for example, this was socialist means of production), and also from the eschatological Utopia (so EU criticizes HU and in turn this criticizes SS'). Without HU, criticism becomes abstract and reformist and turns back into counter-revolution. Without EU, HU becomes fetishistic.

4.1.2   Practical and Constructive Economic-Political Charisms

Charismatic action does not consist only in words, but equally in deeds, in services (I Pet. 4.11). This is now not merely a question of negation of negation, but of affirmation of outgoingness,[20] of the building of a juster system (SS"), of mobilizing the people as protagonist of history (cf. 2.4). And we can still further sub-divide into two categories:

4.1.2.1   Economic-Prophetic Charisms

This category should include all those charisms that promote growth and innovation in man-nature relationships, and in relationships of work and production, which Aristotle called *poiēsis* (*poiēsis kai praxis heteron; EN* 1140–17). Charisms in the economic order are those like the gift of healing (1.4), of miracles (1.5 and 2.4), of helping (2.6), of alms (3.5), works of mercy (3.7) and so on, in St Paul's lists. In terms of our own days, the worker priests come to mind; in the past, the Benedictine monasteries, the Jesuit 'reductions' in Latin America in the seventeenth and eighteenth centuries, and numerous other creative efforts of the Christian conscience through its innovative practices in the economic sphere.

4.1.2.2   Political-Prophetic Charisms

Christians have also become involved charismatically in the political sphere, pushing SS' towards SS" in their very praxis. There was Miguel Hidalgo, a parish priest who organized the popular forces in Mexico for the liberation of their country. The Spanish-dominated bishops excommunicated him, and the theology faculty of Mexico University declared him a heretic, to which his response was that of the Christian hero: 'Open your American eyes; don't let yourselves be misled by your enemies; they are only Catholic in politics; their God is money . . . Do you really think no-one can be a Catholic except through submitting to the Spanish despot? Where did this new dogma, this new article of faith come from? If I had not undertaken this struggle to free our kingdom from the great evils that oppressed it, and the much greater ones that threatened it, I would never have been accused of heresy'.[21] Charismatic political praxis was here taken by the institution and the theologians as heterodoxy. Without wanting to draw too close a parallel, could the case of Camilo Torres, who died like Hidalgo in the failure of his revolutionary attempt, be seen as somewhat similar?

One thinks too of Lacordaire and Lammenais, attacked by a still monarchical Catholicism for speaking of 'Christian democracy'. And, more recently, of the accusations of heterodoxy levelled against the 'Christians for Socialism' by a Catholicism that since *Rerum Novarum* has accepted the basic elements of capitalism, though indulging in reformist criticisms that fail to attack the system, when half the world already lives under socialism. If it is true that the institution holds the *iudicium* (*LG* n. 12), it is equally true that it holds the responsibility for, and is even guilty of, the sin of 'stifling the Spirit' (*ibid.*). Since Joan of Arc, the institution should surely be wary of killing charism—and I am referring to the physical death of charismatics, by no means uncommon in Latin America today.

All the charisms in the Pauline list applied to 4.1.2.1 are applicable here too.

4.1.3   Charisms in Other Religions

Other religions, particularly the Semitic ones, the Indo-European ones rather less and the animistic ones less, clearly also have their prophets who perform their critical-kerygmatic task and carry out their economic and political function. The destitute, disunited Arab tribes of the desert were renewed in a new social structure that flourished for ten centuries. Mahommed, Buddha, Confucius, the Aztec Tlacaelel, all served the world of their time, carrying out a work of charsimatic innovation that in some way served to prepare the way for the Gospel. The Spirit bloweth where it listeth.

4.2   Charisms in the Prophetic Church→Church Sphere

The sacramental, institutional ministry responds to 'Let there be a Church!'; charism responds to: 'Let history march on to the Parousia!' So charismatic activity in the Church should be taken as an *extra,* promoted by the Spirit in order to subvert bureaucratic 'habits' in the structure of the Church. I think one can distinguish at least two types of charism in intra-ecclesial relationships:

4.2.1   Charisms of Ministerial Innovation

Even within ministries, the Spirit calls many ministers to special tasks, to be charismatics within their ministry, without this leading to a confusion between charism and ministry. But one can even subdivide ministerial charisms:

4.2.1.1   Charisms of Founding a Church

Many of the Pauline charisms belong to this category, since his situation was a founding one (apostle 2.1 and evangelist 4.3 principally). Missionaries have this charism: those who founded the Churches in the Mediterranean, in Europe in Russia, in Latin America in the sixteenth century, and in Africa and Asia in the nineteenth.

4.2.1.2   Charisms of Instructing the Faithful

The work of the catechumenate, of catechesis, and much lay action (such as Catholic Action) comes under this heading. In the Pauline list, the relevant types would be: master (2.3), the two kinds of *logos* (1.1 and 1.2), and to a certain extent exhortation (3.4), prophecy (1.6), faith (1.3), tongues (1.8) and the interpretation of tongues (1.9).

4.2.1.3   Charisms of Service to the Community

These refer particularly to the work of various diaconates, such as helping (2.6), alms (3.5), healing (1.4), 'miracles' in the broadest sense (1.5), co-operatives of production or consumption, communities of goods or services, brotherhood in psychological counselling, and so on . . . Services to parishes, to dioceses, to all sorts of ecclesial community—the Church's 'waiting at table'.

4.2.1.4   Charisms of Guiding the Community

There are members of the ministerial institution, such as bishops, who have special charisms of guidance. Helder Camara in Brazil, for example, or Sergio Méndez Arceo in Mexico, or Monsignor Proaño of Riobambia, not to mention Mgr Angelelli of la Rioja (Argentina) who gave his life for the Lord in an assassination carried out by the Argentinian neo-Fascists. Charisms of guidance are mainly discernment of spirits (of the charisms of other members of the community) (1.7), ruling (2.7), pastor (4.4). The ministry is more charismatic when it lets charisms make the Church grow in its other charismatic members.

4.2.2   Non-Ministerial Charisms of Vitalizing the Church

At present, talk of charismatic movements usually refers to some of this type. Yet, as we shall see, this is only a certain well-defined type of charism.

4.2.2.1   Charisms of the Pentecostal or 'Charismatic' Groups

The Spirit has promoted communities or movements of charismatic renewal in the Church, whose vitality and numbers are both on the increase. Particularly linked to the charism of tongues (1.8), ecstasy, trances or simply enthusiasm in prayer and praise-giving, these groups have given new life to the liturgical life of small communities. Such groups, however, have their limitations, as I have already shown in another article in *Concilium*.[22] There are abundant studies on this sort of charism. It must be said that, apart from the Protestant groups (as in Chile where lack of political clarity has led them to organize prayer days for Pinochet!), they are generally groups belonging to the petit-bourgeois classes, without community-existential links in the urban sectors of industrial society. So they totally separate intra-ecclesial revival (with its narcissism and tendency to 'contemplate its own navel', as a Buddhist would say) from prophetic responsibility (cf. 4.1) *outside* the Church.

4.2.2.2   Charisms of the 'Basic Communities'

In a very different way from that prevailing in charismatic movements or religious communities (cf. 4.2.2.3), the 'basic communities' (through their social composition, and their links with the institutional hierarchy, especially in Brazil) possess a charismatic calling devoid of enthusiasms, tongues and extraordinary apparitions, one embedded in the normal daily round of Christian existence and carrying out a deep renewal without making a great deal of noise about it. The 'life revision' (a new version of 'discernment of spirits', 1.7), faith or mutual confidence in the members of the community (1.3) and all services are lived in charity and hope. These base communities today provide the closest analogy with the communities to which Paul wrote: they generate apostles (2.1) and evangelists (4.3), whom they send out to start other communities; they produce their own pastors (4.4) and masters (2.3), and their prophets (1.6). Ther institutional ministry is harmoniously linked to the powers of those members who act on the strength of their own charismatic responsibility. Works of mercy (3.7) are more in evidence than tongues. It is another 'spirit' of the same Spirit.

4.2.2.3   Charisms of Religious Communities

From their outset, with the widows of the early communities or the first Eastern monks of the early fourth century, religious have possessed their own charisms: celibacy or virginity, heroic poverty, service to the poor, contemplation, and so on. This is where the charism of a Benedict, a Francis, a Charles de Foucauld should be placed.

4.2.2.4   Theoretical Charisms

The capacity for theoretical, theological reasoning is also a charism—in the manner of 1.9, 2.3 and in a way 2.2. Karl Rahner has demonstrated the ecclesial and critical relevance of this charism.[23] Latin America today has produced its own brand of critical theology in the 'theology of liberation', but to preach this can lead to persecution and even to assassination attempts, imprisonment and death, inspired not only by the State but also by the institutional ministry. It is true that the Church has the power of 'judgment on the authenticity' of a charism (*LG*), but, as I have already remarked, it also has the responsibility not to 'stifle the Spirit'. In Europe today, theologians can have little idea of the sheer *physical* danger that can be involved in a charismatic call from the Spirit. Writing in 1958, Rahner spoke of the need for freedom of thought in the Church. I am talking of the need to be able to live, physically, once one has uttered the critical prophetic word. But it is in suffering that, after 'testing everything', we learn to 'hold on to what is good' (*LG*. n. 12:1 Thess. 5:12, 19–21).

4.3   Charisms in the 'Social Structure→Future Social Structure' Sphere

The charisms of the Spirit cannot be exhausted in the confines of the Church, nor those of other religions; it blows as much in the world, in particular historical situations, giving rise to heroes, exceptional men who, moved by responsibility for the poor and love for the oppressed, devote their whole lives to preparing for a juster historical kingdom, thereby opening the way to the eschatological Kingdom. Men such as Fidel Castro, Mao, Nyerere—to take one example from many possible in three continents—deserve the closest theological attention. They mobilize their peoples, and the people produce heroes in their midst (cf. 2.4). Their service can be in the ideological sphere (Franz Fanon), the political (Patrice Lumumba) or the economic (Karl Marx). When shall we see the day when the Church's ministry will be capable of forming an adequate judgment on what its Spirit is setting in motion amongst the millions who live in poverty in the Third World? At present, in most of its 'central'—USA, Europe, and so on—social embodiments, and in all those where it is firmly entrenched among the ruling classes—Latin America, Africa—, the Church finds it very difficult to see the charisms of the Spirit at work in men who are neither Christian nor religious—and worse: who are apparently irreligious or atheist. They are certainly atheists of the capitalist fetish—money! Surely they provide the best illustration of how to work for the 'poor of Yahweh' today? But this subject is really too important to be dealt with in one paragraph of an introductory article.

THE INEVITABLE CONFLICT AND DIFFICULTY OF RECONCILING MINISTRY AND CHARISM

In the ultimate Kingdom there will be neither institution nor charism. Once we see God face-to-face there will be no bureaucratic sclerosis, nor any need for charismatic innovation. But in the meantime, in time and history, the Church bears a contradiction (in the real sense of the word) in its essence, whose solution will only be found in the Kingdom. There is a contradiction, an opposition, between its constitutive moments: institution and prophecy. The Church needs an institutional ministry: this is its historical flesh and blood; without the institution there would be neither prophecy nor charism. But when the institution is touched by sin (and being borne by men, it is impossible for it not to be), the contradiction is produced: the institution pronounces charism its enemy. Look at the following example: on 10 May 1977, I read in *Excelsior* (Mexico) that: 'the Cardinal Primate of Colombia and Army General . . . through the organ of the chancellery of the metropolitan Curia, today placed the priest Saturnino Sepúlveda in the hands of military penal justice, for him to be sentenced for subversion, sedition and rebellion'. Leaving aside the truth of the report, and the real motives of both parties (since only God can judge with absolute justice), the example will serve as typical of our time—particularly in the peripheral countries, which suffer the structural injustices exported beyond their frontiers by Europe and the United States. What theological judgment is one to pass on such a situation? What categories should we apply to reflection on ministry and charism in a case like this?

It should be said that the *origin* of a charism is not the same thing as 'judgment of its authenticity'. The verdict of the ministry on a particular charism is not infallible—except in very well-defined cases in which the institution has expressedly used this power. As in the case of Hidalgo (cf., 4.1.2.2), the ministerial authorities are frequently mistaken. This is possible because the Spirit, not the institution, is the origin of charism. Such mistakes do not invalidate the ministry, but they do justify the perseverance of the charismatic, his fidelity to his vocation, so that he can 'test everything and hold on to what is good'.

What happens is that the solidarity often established between members of the institution and the ruling system (such as capitalist means of production) and the dominant classes (such as the bourgeoisie of the dependent nations), can only lead to conflict with the Christian charismatic committed to the oppressed classes (such as the peasants, the unemployed or the urban proletariat) and to a different means of production. There is then a double risk in being a prophet: *from the Church*, of persecution by an institution compromised with the existing social structure (as in 4.2.2.2), but also, and more radically, *from the world*, of being repressed by the State, which is both dependent on the system and the oppressor, at least in Latin America, as in shown by the case from *Excelsior* and the type of charism analyzed in 4.1.

The 'death risk' inherent in the charismatic calling on its prophetic level (4.1), as for the thousands of Christians who died in the Roman circuses, and the thousands more who today suffer imprisonment, torture and death for their faith in Latin America, is part of the essence of charismatic praxis. The persecution of the just redounds to the Glory of the Infinite. The saddest aspect—though understandable—is that it should have to do so with the blessing of the ecclesial ministry. In any event, the sufferings of the just, and their blood, become one with the Lamb that was slain and go to build the heavenly Jerusalem. The Beast and the Dragon will not prevail against them. Faith in the Church encourages those who are called to all-out responsibility for the poor, the 'other', to continue in their painful mission. Beyond the prophet's curse on the day he was born echoes the call to renewal and innovation, the call of hope: 'Come, Lord Jesus!'

Translated by Paul Burns

Notes

1. There is a short bibliography in H. Küng, 'The Charismatic Structure of the Church', in *Concilium* 4 (1965), n. 7. Biblical dictionaries, such as Kittel, *ThWNT*, give indications under words such as *charisma, pneumatika, diakonia, energmata,* etc.

Also worthy of note are: H. Leclerq, *DACL* III/I (1913), pp. 579–98; L. Lemonnyer, *DBS* I (1928), pp. 1233–4; J. Geweiss and K. Rahner, *LTK* II (1958), pp. 1025–30; X. Ducros, *DSp* II (1953), pp. 503–7; general tables in *DTC* (1953), pp. 582–3; E. Bettencourt in *Sacramentum Mundi* I (London & New York, 1968), pp. 283–4, with a bibliography. See also, B. Maréchaux, *Les charismes du Saint Esprit* (Paris, 1921); F. Prat, *La théologie de St Paul* I (Paris[17], 1930); E. B. Allo, *Première Epître aux Corinthiens* (Paris, 1934), pp. 317–86; E. Kaesemann, 'Amt und Gemeinde im Neuen Testament', in *Exegetische Versuche und Besinnungen* I (Gottingen, 1960), pp. 109 ff. There are few studies of later periods: see A. Ritter, *Charisma im Verstaendnis des Johannes Chrysostomos* (Gottingen, 1972). Worth remembering is K. Rahner, *The Dynamic Element in the Church* (London & New York, 1959); also K. Schwarzwaeller, 'Kirche und Prophetie', in *Evang. Theol.* 26 (1966), pp. 590–96; W. Garret, *Charisma. A Study in the Legitimation of Values* (Diss. Drew Univ., 1968); G. Hasenhuettl, 'Die Charismen im Leben der Kirche', in *Der Seelsorge* 39 (1969), pp. 167–74 (cf. *Charisma, Ordnungsprinzip der Kirche,* Freiburg, 1969). The review *Foi et Vie* devoted its number 4/5 (1973) to the subject, with articles by L. Dallière, J. Serr, M. Harper and others; as did the review *Christus* (Mexico) its number 475 (1975), with articles by S. Galilea and others. From Latin America, there is J. Marins, *Carismas y carismáticos en la comunidad eclesial* (Bogotá, 1976), and L. Boff, 'Eclesiogénesis, las comunidades de base re-inventan la Iglesia', in *Servir* (65/66 (Mexico. 1976), pp. 401–6. Official texts to be consulted are *Mystici Corporis,* in *AAA* 35 (1943), p. 200 ff, and, from the Second Vatican Council, *LG* nn. 12 and 4; *AA* nn. 3 and 30; *AG* nn. 4–32.

2. Cf. *DTC* V, 1823; VI, 1158; VIII, 1315, and so on.

3. *Op. cit.*

4. *Ibid.,* c. 595.

5. H. Küng, *op. cit.,* p. 57.

6. *LG* n. 12. The same traditional division is found in most of the works mentioned (e.g., X. Ducros, p. 504).

7. V. Cosmão, 'Charismatiques et politiques', in *Foi et développement* 26 (1975), c. 1.

8. Cf. M. Weber, *On Charisma and Institution-Building,* ed. S. Eisenstadt, (Chicago, 1968).

9. *The Social System,* ch. 8 (London, 1951), pp. 249 ff.

10. *Ibid.,* ch. XI, p. 480 ff, particularly par. 2, 'The ascendancy of the charismatic revolutionary movement' (p. 520): Parsons says that, 'a general theory of the processes of change of social systems is not possible in the present state of knowledge' (p. 486). What he cannot conceive is a 'process of change of the systems as systems', (*Ibid.*)—but this is precisely the problem that concerns the theology of liberation!

11. Cf. Samir Amin, *Le développement inégal* (Paris, 1973).

12. 'Et eadem ratione . . . est inter eos dominativum iustum', II–II, q. 57, a. 4, resp.

13. Sp. Ed. *Morfología del Cuento* (Madrid, 1973).

14. *Semantique structurale* (Paris, 1966).

15. 'Cláusula del Testamento', in *Obras escogidas de B. de las Casas,* vol. V (Madrid, 1958), p. 539.

16. *Ibid.,* pp. 539–40.

17. *Ibid.*

18. *Ibid.*

19. *Op. cit.,* p. 540.

20. See my article 'Domination-Liberation', par. 6, in *Concilium* 96 (1974).

21. *Colección de documentos sobre la guerra de la Independencia en Mexico (1808–1821),* ed. Hernández and Dávalos (Mexico, 1877), p. 73.

22. 'The Base in the Theology of Liberation', in *Concilium* 104 (1975).

23. *Op. cit.,* pt II.

Luigi Sartori

The Structure of Juridical and Charismatic Power in the Christian Community

A POSSIBLE AMBIGUOUS CONFRONTATION

NOWADAYS much writing of a socio-political nature is published on the Church and the whole Christian world.[1] This can be useful and to the point; it can assist the confrontation between the world and the Church; furthermore, it makes plain the common ground of Christianity and history. Along with a great deal else in modern culture, the polarity of the argument offers genuine and fruitful criteria in the field of knowledge, and guarantees close consideration of whatever is under review. When a subject is isolated from its context one runs the risk of not understanding it fully, because every matter is only real in so far as one can see where it comes from and where it is going to: its growth, associations and antici-pated polarities.

It is clear from a study of the past that there have always been tensions inside the Church; and also that it has been customary to make reference to a system of theoretical justifications which supports now this side and now that of the argument. The habit of referring to politi-cal categories is a much more recent phenomenon. From the very beginning Protestantism has maintained a position which is simply that of opposing the Gospel to the tangible structure of the Church (the Pope, for example). This point of view is basic to a view of 'the spiritual and invisible Church' which is contrasted with the 'visible Church'. In the twentieth century, 'charism' is thought of as the opposite of an institution; this has came about because the argument has been taken up by everyone, laymen included; it has moved out of the field of purely theological discussion and into the story of human rights (R. Sohm) and even more into sociology (Weber).[2] One might even say that 'liberty versus authority' is a more appropriate summary of the discussion.

With due respect to this socio-political material and its value, it is a good idea to turn to theology on this question even if there is a danger of utopian solutions.

There is a danger inherent in the former literature: that of debasing certain theological concepts. 'Charism' cannot be equated with 'liberty' and thus be set against authority; nor can it be thought of as 'spontaneity' and as an alternative to the rule of law and order; nor can it cover the whole area of pluralism and be placed in opposition to the 'judiciary' as synonymous with unity and uniformity; still less can one refer to the 'divine' or the 'Spirit' as if the structure either of the law or of any other institution were 'human' or the 'flesh'.

However, no more can the judiciary think of itself as an institution or a structure, or in terms of 'visibility'. Current ideas of power have led to its spread beyond politics and the law; power can mean the ability to bring pressure in secret behind the scenes; that power belongs to ideology and to the manipulative process exercised by the mass media, the 'imperialism of money' (as Pius XI calls it in *Quadragesimo Anno*); and that, in turn, controls many other forms of power.

Theologians ought to begin by clarifying the problem, even before they put the judiciary and 'charism' in opposite camps. The very word 'charism' hints at poverty and isolation as if it were a tiny David facing Goliath—an unarmed man confronting a breast-plated giant. One associates the judiciary with a structure and with power automatically in a way which is impossible in connexion with 'charism'.[3] Perhaps this relies on an unconscious wish to bring a value judgment (drawn from a reading of the Bible) to bear on the confrontation between 'charism' and the law so as to aggrandize the victory given to the one who was indisputably on God's side.

Nowadays one can confirm not only that charismatics have their place in the structure of a community but that there are genuine principles for building a 'charismatic structure'.[4] Even official theological pronouncements incorporate these ideas. Pius XII's encyclical *Mystici Corporis* (1943) opposes a running down of the 'organic structure' of the Church both in the hierarchic and in the charismatic ('minime reputandum est, hanc ordine digestam seu "organicam", ut aiunt, Ecclesiae corporis structuram solis hierarchiae gradibus absolvi ac definiri, vel, ut opposita sententia tenet, unice ex charismaticis constare' (Denz/Sch.

3801). This is the first instance to admit that charismatics belong to the structure of the Church, although it does not place them in opposition to the hierarchy.

The word 'structure' means the visible 'body' of the Church—the historical form in which the mystery of the Church was made manifest. However, it also carries further implications; one could call it an organization which creates harmony between differing parties and results in a dynamic unity. The Christian community, therefore, derives its essential principle of life and unity from the hierarchy; yet not only from it, but from the charismatic as well.

Futhermore, it has become a commonplace to talk about the 'sacramental structure' of the Church and to refer to the sacraments as fundamental to order and structure in the community. The problem has increased in complexity.[5] Theological thinking has to take account of three separate factors, structurally speaking (perhaps, even, of three separate structures); these are: authority, the charismatic and the sacraments. That is, there are at least three; there may be yet another unexplored field of factors as yet outside the province of the Church but like seeds waiting to be developed within it. They will bear fruit in ecumenical and missionary advances and are moral values which come into the Church through culture and the great religions—it may be that this new field, which has so far been merely touched on by some progressive modes of thought in theology, perhaps constitutes a fourth group of structural factors.[6] Is the Church simply the result of what has taken place in the past? Is it the outcome of the greatness of the risen Christ? Is it not also composed of what lies ahead for it, yet to be revealed by future history?

To return to the connexion between authority and charism, we note that the echo still lingers in Vatican II of the discussion in *Mystici Corporis,* despite the rush to smooth things over.[7] At the roots of the tension there is a view of charism which associates it with 'miracles' and strange events. On the rare occasions through the ages when the Magisterium spoke of charisms, it referred to them as though they were exceptional, privileged; and always did so in terms proper to a miracle and the sanctity of saints who are canonized, or about to be. The passage quoted from *Mystici Corporis* ends with a statement that 'amazing gifts have never been lacking in the Church'. Nowadays the miraculous is not acceptable as proof in apologetics, and all theology in recent centuries until Vatican II, especially thinking about the Church, was dominated by apologetic concerns. Consolidation and not renewal was important. The call to Christ, to Jesus as founder, turns principally on the defence of bishops and of order, which 'ex intentione Dei' must remain unchanged. The Holy Spirit, who may instigate miracles, and, of course, the saints only have the task of 'confirming', by means of apologia, what has already been established by Christ, which is the basic structure; and that cannot become a principle of disorder.

The real problem is thus one of ideas about the Holy Spirit and Christ; it is the central problem of Christology. The discussion hinges upon unity or division in Christ; concentration on any one aspect reduces attention paid to another and destroys unity. By making the charismatic mysterious and sacred it enlarges the distance between it and the Church and alienates it from Christ, the divine and the Spirit. It is essential to bring all elements together in an ordered structure.[8]

WHAT THE NEW TESTAMENT HAS TO TELL US

There is no question of the Bible being considered in its entirety here, only those aspects of it which are relevant to the matter in hand.

The Messianic Age and the Age of the Total Manifestation of the Spirit

It is not possible to put the Old Testament and the New Testament in opposite corners too categorically, as if one represented the 'letter', the law and the institution while the other stood for the 'spirit', liberty and charism. It is true, however, that theologians, particularly followers of St Paul, see things in terms of opposing forces. At that time the Spirit was meted out with reserve whereas now the Spirit is given in full measure (cf. John 3:34).

Nor must one refer exclusively to the role of the prophets. In point of fact, they often attacked existing institutions in Israel, although not necessarily on their own account. Moreover there was a certain amount of institutionalization in any prophesying. Schools of thought grew up round the prophets themselves. The age saw the follower turn himself increasingly from the charismatic to the study and the search for wisdom. Nor is it enough to idealize (as von Rad does) the period of Judges, during which Israel was open to the future of a theocracy which was almost totally lacking in a mediating structure.[9] Despite the fact that Jewish institutional structures derive from Moses both before and after his death, he is, nevertheless, the prototype of a charismatic man: the faultless prophet down to his gift of a new eschatological prophet. Every subsequent spread of the power can be described as a 'communication' and as 'participation' (cf. the account of the seventy elders in Numbers: 'and I will take of the spirit which is upon thee, and will put it upon them . . . and took of the spirit that was upon him, and gave it to the seventy elders': 11:17, 25).

However, the gift of the Spirit is only sent down in abundance through Christ in the New Testament (I Thess. 1:5). Jesus was able to reassure them: 'He that believeth in me, the works that I do shall he do also; and greater works than these shall he do' (John 14:12). Peter's first speech at Pentecost recognized the fact that Joel's prophecy had come to pass in the messianic age: '. . . and your sons and daughters shall prophesy and your young men shall see visions and your old men shall dream dreams' (Acts 2:17–21). Pentecost was not a unique event—it was repeated; see Acts 6 (Stephen); 8 (Philip); 9 (Saul); 10 (Cornelius); 19 (Ephesus); and so on.

The Spirit and the Spirit of Christ

The Bible tells us that the great gift, the rich gift which the Father gave to the world is Jesus Christ (cf. John 1:16–17; Rom. 5:15) Jesus is the One on whom the Spirit descended, according to the prophet Isaiah. Jesus said so himself in the first place, according to Luke 4:17–21, and it is in him that the Spirit is given 'but not by measure' (John 3:34).

This all takes place during 'the era of incarnation'. Paul, the theologian of the new Christianity, invites a faith in 'Christ in the flesh' and in the law of being made flesh which leads to the Cross, inevitably. What is new and unrepeatable in the Christian era is still hidden in history and awaits its complete manifestation. Christ's second coming is by no means of secondary importance in the Gospel. In certain ways, therefore, Christ is still buried in history, even within the Church where he awaits his resurrection, or, perhaps more correctly, his epiphany (within the confines of history).

We find evidence of an awareness of the profound spirit of unity between the Holy Spirit and Christ early on in the New Testament. Jesus is acknowledged by reference to the Old Testament. His triumph is also regarded as a completion. The transition from synagogue to church is brought about by structures modelled on methods known to the ancients and that encouraged the development of new systems taken from Greco-Roman culture. A pronouncement in accordance with the biblical canon is of fundamental importance when one is confronted by evangelism and spiritualism which are Manichean in origin and which reject the 'flesh' in favour of the spirit.

The same apostolic note is struck by the Church when affirming the lastingness of the state of 'kenosis' in the Church even after Christ, or possibly of the eternity of Incarnation. The Church is, nevertheless, based in human history and is to be found in history. While 'unity' and 'sanctity' can be regarded as giving weight to eschatological 'glory', the word 'apostolic' suggest humility and weakness rather than the miraculous. Apostles, prophets, learned doctors . . . and all the other 'gifted ones' who make up the structure of the Church (cf. the list in I Cor. 12: 28–30 and Eph. 4:2) seem to come down from on high and derive from Christ, but they are also historical events and prolong the visible existence of an historical Jesus incarnate.[10]

On the other hand, the distance between Christ and the church allows the Church to see itself as perpetually in need of purification and of teaching. In that sense, one permanently travels the road which leads from the letter of the law to a state of grace. It is not just the path of the liturgy; it is real. The father of all the gifted—Paul—was the first to battle against the illusions held by those charismatics who dreamed of being able to do without rules, thus risking their own frailty and ignoring their own weaknesses.

Incorporating the Charismatic

Christ is the word made flesh in Jesus of Nazareth; but he is also the word made manifest in creation. Christ's gifts are handed down by history in their true colours and result in human creativity. Paul reacted sharply (cf. I Cor. 12–14) to the tendency both to limit freedom in favour of a single monopolizing gift and to the tendency to give privileges to the charismatic, which causes alienation and evasions. In the catalogue of the charismatic he lists the humdrum duties which are part of the everyday life of the community (help for the poor, consoling the bereaved, exhortation, the hearing of catechisms). The ebullient charismatics are only half so, because they lack the gift of interpretation; the gift of speaking with many tongues, ecstatically, is not of practical use in the community—the hallmark of the truly charismatic.[11]

The preference Paul gives to the gift of prophecy ought to be seen in the light of this problem. He would prefer everyone to prophesy, and in such a way as to elicit the approval of everyone when they listen to the one who is actually speaking and making his own contribution to the development of the community in faith.[12] Up to this point in time there can be no union between the Spirit (the gift of the Spirit—'pneuma') with 'understanding' ('nous', Paul calls it). Until the gift which comes from Christ enters a person and makes him human, until then he is not incarnate in the human gift, nor is it constructive to the Church. ('I will pray with the spirit and I will pray with the understanding also . . . Yet in the Church I had rather speak five words with my understanding that I might teach others also, than ten thousand words in an unknown tongue'. I Cor. 14: 15–19)

In the light of this statement one can see why Paul included the gift of influencing others in the list of gifts; it was because he made us of his charism as apostle even when he was meting out rules and regulations; summoning up real power (the judiciary, as we say now). It is why he made an explicit appeal to the criterion of 'order and 'propriety' in the life of the community (cf. I Cor. 14:40).

To sum up, one can analyze Paul's observations on the charismatic as follows; he wanted to stress the richness of Christ made manifest, and space to be made for everyone, above all the poor, those who may possibly be overlooked and despised ('idioti', in the original Greek): those who are unable to make any contribution whatever beyond saying 'amen' frequently and with understanding. By means of the metaphor of the human body Paul is able to show the value of the less noble charisms to the others (I Cor. 12: 22–6).[13]

The Ultimate Gift

Just as each gift comes from the Spirit and they live together in unity at the source, so the gift in the world merges into the new body of Christ which is the community, the Church. Why does Paul insist on his many and diverse forms of 'charism', on the role of authority, on the importance of openness to each other, and of decency and order? It is because the true gift that the Father wants to bestow upon the world is, and always was, Jesus Christ; and the body of Christ is made up of the Church as it in turn is made up of every Christian community.

What Paul secretly wanted, in his heart of hearts, can be seen from Ephesians 4:11, with its list of the charismatic; it is essential to integrate the faithful (the saints) because each one has his proper function and each one contributes to the body of Christ. Each one is special, according to his gift, even if it is 'meted out' as the text says.

Missionary activity is thus essential; the growth of each one increases the Church because this is the way to go on giving the gift of Christ to man.[14]

Paul says that charity is the greatest gift of all when he speaks of gifts in the thirteenth chapter of I Corinthians. The first duty of any authority must be, as Paul showed in his actions, to reorganize the activity of all the members, to administer to the needs of the poorest and to make for change and development. In other words, to give life to charity as a spirit and in each and every one in the community because it is only in this way that the gift becomes real. An act of love, a Church which reveals itself as a gift of love from the father, is not merely a human fact or a historical institution.

The Bible has no 'abstract' arguments with 'liberty' on one side and 'authority' on the other. There are formalities and absolutes which lie between liberty and authority. On the other hand, the call of Christ and the Spirit indicates the value of the Father's gift which is offered to all men in one Man, through whom is transmitted the visible charity which makes the Church and makes for a Church which operates as a visible charity.

CONCLUSION

The foregoing observations are intended to help us find our way towards a solution of ways in which to solve the question of juridical and charismatic power. Above all, it is necessary to emphasize the fact that they have common ground—the charismatic is fundamental to every-thing that has been built ecclesiastically. Let us go back to the discussion of the three structures (*juridical*—the *sacramental*—the *charismatic*); it is possible to come to the following conclusions briefly (apart from the fact that this is not the place for lengthy proofs); basically, everything is a gift, 'charism'—the structure of the Church is conceived charismatically because the 'call' came even before the sacrament (each one has his own 'name' everlastingly—that is what predestination means); thus the structure can be defined as sacramental because God's gifts are taken over, integrated, directed, and consecrated by actual historical events, analogies to those which organize the whole gift—that is, Christ—which blesses them, makes them official and binds them to the source—Christ—and makes use of them within the Church; ultimately, it created the juridical structure which in fact controls the 'viability' of the gifts and of the sacraments. There are three structures, like three moments or levels of a single structure. The subordination of the juridical to the sacramental can be seen as a doctrine of pacification. On the other hand, it is not true to say that the juridical and the sacramental are based in the charismatic.[15] It is harder to detect the root of authority in the area of 'charism', not least in the vocabulary.[16] Nowadays discussion of the role of its servants helps to set in order the movement from the general to the specific; charism implies something very general, and within that general category are to be found the various subdivisions of ministers, or those whose function it is to carry out necessary tasks among which one can list authority and the need for government.

Charism as an Aid to Judgment

As we have seen, every gift is *apriori* rooted in a human being, and it must be judged and welcomed, if possible, by every discerning per-son.[17] It is a question of realising that what a man offers is not simply a human gift but a gift from the risen Christ and his spirit; it is a matter of meshing it in with other gifts and of merging it with the 'greatest of those' which is charity so as to stimulate and inspire it; it is a case of it bearing fruit which will build the body of Christ, or the Church. One must pray for guidance from the Father of lights to do this; one must glorify and give thanks to God, the great Giver; one must offer up each gift as though it were the gift of all, from the whole community in his name. This task of active or passive judgment must be brought to every gift and is particularly important when it comes to the gift of authority which is in charge of the duty of circulating and redeploying these gifts, and which is the method of 'judgment'. A proper discernment of these gifts is important because it calls upon the community to act decisively and solemly in the invocation of the Spirit and the laying on of hands, which confirms one of God's acts (this is the sacrament of order in the Catholic Church, as it is in other churches).

What is the Hallmark of the Gift of Authority?

The answer to this question lies in what was said earlier. Authority exists to embody charity as the soul of every gift and as a way of communicating and harmonizing all the contributions and as a way of building the body of Christ. In more universal and abstract terms, it is the gift which unifies and ensures the harmony of the entire community. Seen in conjunction with charity, as it is, it is a humble but glorious gift. Charity only becomes visible in acts (real love is only expressed in acts, and the most concrete are the most real). To judge by these standards authority has nothing of its own to offer and is only to be considered according to the gifts which the community possesses and is rich in so far as it has been able to marshal them. Authority cannot create gifts, nor does it give birth to them, in the strictest sense. Its work is to attend manifestations and work for the harmony of all. Authority as a gift is an empty shape which is filled in by what it orders—that is, all the other gifts.[18] One who is not gifted himself to serve the gifted. He ought to feel the joy of searching, discovering and evaluating gifts, of defending and making them available as though they were his own. There is an urgent need to harmonize all gifts in true ecclesiastical form all over the world so that the greatest wealth shall be allied to the greatest need.

No one can claim a monopoly, not even that of claiming to stand for Christ or the Spirit, no more than any single person can claim judgment.

All that goes to make up reality in the Church is entrusted to authority as it guides it towards unity. A certain formalism, familiar by now to us, is of assistance in the duty of deciding who should have power in the Church, who has a genuine call, and who is fit to guide others. It is only by respecting others, the weaker and less gifted, and helping them to value their gifts that we will arrive at a unity and freedom from waste (even to 'gather up the fragments' Jn. 6:12). Only those who show the patience over a long period needed to deal with the tension which arises in the search for unity, and only they if they act without resorting to a preordained scheme can be said to be truly those with the 'call' or the 'charism' of authority.

Institutions are the means whereby the many may participate in the gifts of the few; they help because liberty is nourished by charity and becomes a gift, one of the outward signs of a Church which has always shown the fatigue and the joys of the 'harvest' or 'treasure' in eschatological terms and which now looks forward to the future in which every good thing will come to us through Christ.

Translated by Alison Weir

Notes

1. This can most readily be seen in the 'basic communities' and 'informal groups'. Cf. 'Les communautés de base', in *Lumière et vie,* no. 19 (1970) and *Concilium,* 2 (1975).

2. H. von Campenhausen refers to the Weberian category in the first few pages of his *Kirchliches Amt und geistliche Vollmacht in den ersten drei Jahrhunderten* (Tübingen, 1963). See G. Hasenhüttl on the discussion between A. Harnack and R. Sohm in *Charisma. Ordnungsprinzip der Kirche* (Freiburg, 1969). P. Boglioni's essay 'The charismatic in the life of the mediaeval Church' in *Sacra Doctrina* 59 (1970), pp. 383–430 is valuable in that he uses the Weberian category.

3. From a seminar held in an Italian 'basic community' on the question of authority as 'charism'.

4. H. Küng and G. Hasenhüttl agree on charismatic structure.

5. *Lumen Gentium* ch. 2 proposes the formula of 'the sacramental structure' of the Church.

6. Cf. my article 'The Church' in the *Theological Dictionary* edited by Bauer and Molari (Assisi, 1974) in which I describe four aspects of the church: the juridical, sacramental, the charismatic and the missionary.

7. It is interesting to note that Vatican II uses a wealth of biblical vocabulary: 'gifts, donations, thanks, operations, strengths, ministrations, servitude . . .' These terms are mixed with scholastic and contemporary vocabulary. It

is noticeable that the use of the word 'ministry' is made equivalent to 'priestly ministry and hierarchical function'.

8. *Lumen Gentium* no. 12 is particularly important because it sanctions the idea of the charismatic as normal within the Church.

9. Cf. G. von Rad, *Theologie des Alten Testaments* (Munich, 1962 & 1965).

10. It is interesting that the three synonymous terms charisms, administrations, operations' of I Cor. 12:4–6, refer to Jesus as administrator and almost imply 'Servant of God.'

11. Cf. I Cor. 14:27–8. If there was no 'interpreter' they were to keep silent in the Church.

12. 'You may all prophesy, one at a time'.

13. Witness the attention Paul paid to the 'weak' who could so easily be offended. Cf. I Cor. 8:11–12.

14. The idea of 'profit' come within that of charism: 'But the manifestation of the spirit is given to every man to profit withal.' But Paul also had in mind a community which could be of profit to unbelievers.

15. One way in which the sacramental is subordinated to the juridical is to be found in *Lumen Gentium,* particularly in no. 21, where the roots of the nature of the magisterium and priestly government by the pastors are essentially sacramental.

16. See *Lumen Gentium* 4 (and a similar passage in 7), which deals with 'hierarchical and charismatic gifts.

17. When discussing the ideal situation in which 'all are prophets', Paul warns: 'Let the prophets speak two or three and let the others judge' (I Cor. 14:29). But he told the community at Corinth that the community had to shoulder the responsibility of judging.

18. See Rahner's essay in the section 'Charism' in *Sacramentum Mundi* or in *Lex. f. Theol. u. Kir.* and in *The Dynamic Element in the Church,* (London, 1961), according to which the institution is the means whereby a gift can be made available to all because, although it is unique, it can still be shared.

Raul Vidales

Charisms and Political Action

IT is now clear that the charismatic phenomenon inspired by Pentecostalism is wider than the institutional framework of the various Churches and reveals even greater socio-political implications that involve it in the complex panorama of present-day society. The point at issue is not so much the climate of tolerance and acceptance—extraordinary though this is—shown to it within the Churches, nor the contradictions it has engendered within the Churches, but mainly what this theoretical-practical concept of Christianity can mean as a response to the serious demands made on Christianity by the present historical situation.

The phenomenon has awakened the interest of pastors and theologians, of social scientists and politicians; analysis and diagnosis take their tone from their starting-point; either in judgment of what the movement means as a 'current of renewal' within the Church, or what its implications are as an element that in fact sustains the *status quo*.

Without claiming to make an exhaustive examination, I would like to start by setting this phenomenon within the context provided by the present phase of multi-national capitalism as a determining element in the situation of Latin American countries. An inter-disciplinary analysis would require consideration of many complex elements in order to reach a better understanding of the phenomenon; therefore I propose only to put forward a few judgments which have arisen from an 'action-reflection' carried out from within a particular process and a specific historical context.

Analysis and understanding of this phenomenon would have to be approached in different ways in the major power blocs and in the dependent countries; my analysis starts from the reality of the latter, although the appearance and growth of neo-Pentecostalism in the industrialized countries—and particularly among the middle and upper classes there—has broken the classic mould in which this type of phenomenon belonged to the lower levels of society. We cannot just affirm that in both cases this phenomenon obeys the same laws of conditioning, or has the same significance, much less that it fulfills the same function.

Consequently, to view the phenomenon from the point of view of the dependent countries implies taking up an epistemological position; it implies a scientific as well as a theological choice. My subject then will be the subject of neo-Pentecostalism in Latin America particularly among Catholics and in so far as it relates to the popular classes.

THE RESPONSE FROM THE CHURCHES

One of the most significant elements in the progress made by the Churches during the last few years is their growing sensitivity to world problems. Events take place that require an historical response on the part of the Churches and they are seen as such, but when one talks of a 'response from the Churches', it is clear that not all members of the Churches are involved. We know that within the Churches different groups have been formed to fulfil significant functions; there are others who have maintained a frankly reactionary attitude in politics, clinging to conservative ideological outlooks and 'traditional' religious practices, and such groups are frequently bound up with the power structure in a given country. There are also those who put forward a third way of change, based on democratic order inspired by Christian principles, as an alternative between capitalism and socialism. These groups are imbued with bourgeois ideology disguised as reforming zeal and absorb a series of ethical but abstract values, such as 'liberty,' 'participation', 'democracy', and so on. Their ideological strength stems from the postulate that the class struggle, since it is fed by hate and leads to violence (violence which would be provoked by the oppressed!), is incompatible with the Gospel. In the end, though, their criticism fails to reach the roots of the unjust system they claim they wish to reform. There are also those who have shown themselves fully committed to building a new society and a new man fully involved in the political struggle for liberation, because they see this as the historical expression of their faithfulness to the Spirit; they further the project of making the Church show a new face, based on commitment to 'the least of the brethren'.

The response the Church is making to these central problems is therefore varied from country to country and within each country; it is polarized to the extent that the Churches themselves reflect the global contradictions of the social system, but the most significant fact in Latin America is the presence of ever-growing sections of the people who demonstrate an increasing collective will for politically expressed liberation; they are ordinary people, still bound to rudimentary forms of religious experience, but to the extent that they become the subject of their own liberation they place themselves in the position of being able to reformulate their experience of the faith and their reflection of it.

These ingredients make appreciation of the Pentecostal phenomenon far more complex. Nevertheless, one can still give voice to some general suspicions that will determine the broad lines of our enquiry.

PENTECOSTALISM IN THE LATIN AMERICAN CONTEXT

The phenomenon of Pentecostalism should be clearly situated in the overall context affecting the dependent countries and seen in relation to the specific characteristics of the present phase of international capitalism.

In the last few years the contradictions in the evolution of Latin America have become more acute. The crisis of international capitalism has had serious repercussions on the working classes of the industrialized nations, but even more serious ones on the exploited masses of the dependent countries. The unequal and contradictory nature of world expansion of capitalism today has produced an economic recession which in turn brings grave consequences such as inflation, unemployment and hunger, which reduce the over-exploited majorities of the poor countries to literally sub-human levels. The present phase of capitalism is based particularly on an ever-increasing concentration of capital and technology, which facilitates the enormous extraction of profits from the dependent countries, exploitation of their work forces and indiscriminate manipulation of credit. This has led to the creation of new centres of economic and political power which are superior even to national governments. We now know of the existence of international minorities allied to the 'establishment' of different countries who exercise economic, political and ideological power at the expense of exploited majorities.

These minorities, working with central government, are no longer interested in so-called modern democracy and freedom because whenever a formal or representative democracy ceases to work for the system, a way seems to be found for transition to fascist-type authoritarian and totalitarian systems. Once this happens, the social order is subjected to new norms and laws; individual rights and freedoms are suppressed, as are political freedoms and trade union rights and new methods of control are imposed—persecution, prison, torture, exile and execution. The pattern that multi-national capitalism is forcing on the dependent countries is characterized by internal forms of subversion, economic and political de-stabilization, and a vast panoply of ideological struggle.

In the face of an overall situation like this the classic questions posed by critics of religion come once more to the fore. In the case of Pentecostalism one has to ask what role the charismatic phenomenon inspired by Pentecostalism plays, not only within the Churches but more importantly, as an attitude taken by the Churches to the historical tasks involved in building a new society as an alternative to the system of domination. What role can it play in the process of liberating the oppressed?

SOCIOLOGICAL OBJECTIONS

It would seem therefore that one has to sow at least some seeds of doubt on the value of this movement from a sociological standpoint. Elsewhere I have pointed out that modern sociological analysis of the religious phenomenon is inclined towards a sociology of past structures or of an organization based on structural economic relationships. The problem can be posed in the following way: what ties are there between relationships of meaning and relationships of power in a given society, since the 'power' relationship is linked with structural situations on the economic level and the 'meaning' relationship is linked to meanings on the symbolical level, which give their identity to social agents?

The theoretical postulates for an examination of this problem would seem to be: on one hand the 'socio-genesis' of the religious phenomenon ('moments of effervescence', utopian and messianic social protest movements), the material basis of ideas, religion as ideology, and the Church as ideological apparatus of the state or of a particular class; on the other hand the postulate of the 'supply and demand' of religious agents and the theory of the ideological class struggle. Given this perspective, what one has to ask in the context of a dependent social structure is: what place is there for ideology in general, and religious ideology in particular, within such a structure? In our particular case, the question has to be particularized to bring in the specific case of Pentecostalism. One can then ask: what mechanisms have reciprocal incidence on the content of a symbolical system, its organization and the class structure? This means that analysis of this religious phenomenon has also to involve analysis of the type of society within which it appears, its economic base, its power structure and the type of ideology that sustains it. The other side of the examination is then a religious 'supply and demand' situation, the structure of religious practices and the specific function that the religious phenomenon exercises as doctrinal justification.

I propose to use two working hypotheses in order to pursue this examination:

(a) Religious practice effectively becomes an alienating factor within the overall framework of dependent capitalist structure, particularly amongst the traditionally exploited working classes, who have little or no historical and political consciousness and hardly any active participation in transforming the ruling system. To the extent that religious practice contributes to the maintenance of a mythical, a-historical and a-political consciousness, it sacralizes the established order and in the end becomes one element that keeps the establishment in its place. This is where theoretical and practical objections to the particular form taken by Christianity in the case of Pentecostalism come into play, because Pentecostalism exercises a considerable influence over the groups that practise it. It encourages individualistic and inward-looking codes and practices of behaviour. In this way, basic elements of the faith such as 'unity', 'peace', 'order', 'freedom', 'the will of God', and so on, become channels for the introduction of ideological elements that serve to legitimize the established order. In these conditions, the religious phenomenon is liable to be taken over and manipulated by the ruling system—the system of domination.

This helps us to understand why the adherents of this type of religious practice are incapable of formulating an historical account of the subversive dialectic of the values of freedom they purport to believe in. This is the failure that leads to the operation of 'religious inversion of the system', because if the system needs to legitimize itself and needs to assure itself that it is serving democracy, freedom, humanization, and so on, it can find both its 'requisite criticism' and at the same time its greatest support in a religious phenomenon that only criticizes 'excesses'. The use the system makes of certain religious rites, symbols and practices—particularly in the way of religious and civil official ceremonies—is not so important as, on a deeper level, its borrowing, utilization and finally exploitation of the symbolical universe of the popular classes. This is what underlies what has been called 'the disposable cultural surplus' which has to be redeemed for and by the people.

(b) Yet we have already seen that the most significant phenomenon of the last few years of Latin American history is the uprising of the popular classes assuming the project of their own liberation. Experience and studies in this field lead to a second ground for objection, namely: the characteristics of the religious practice of the exploited classes who call themselves Christian, to the extent that they take on and live their faith in a dialectical relationship with the process of liberation, are a recovery of the subversive and 'protestant' (utopian) potential of religion, its power to play an active role in, and make an effective contribution to, the task of the revolutionary transformation of society. These characteristics can be seen above all in groups who make use of all the help they need to question and reformulate their religious understanding and practice, at the same time as they further their social commitment. These would not seem to be the characteristics of Pentecostalism.

PENTECOSTALISM IN A CONTEXT OF OPPRESSION

A closer look at the charismatic Pentecostal phenomenon, particularly in Latin America, allows the following considerations:

(a) In common with other so-called 'renewal' movements, this phenomenon did not arise from within the dependent conditions of Latin America, so the first question to ask is to what extent this religious phenomenon has been able to establish a genuine relationship between those who practice it and their real conditions of existence, not only as individuals but also as members of the overall society. If religion operates as a 'power system', what role does Pentecostalism play in a context of oppression? What does it offer its adherents in the way of means to action, and to what type of action? The answers to these questions are not easy but I think we can provide at least some of their elements.

Personal observation and studies made of this subject suggest that the basic characteristics of the Pentecostalist phenomenon are the following: individualism, cultivation of certain inner values and moments of religious enthusiasm. It sees itself as a reforming religious movement centred on personal renewal. It offers peace of mind and a remedy for the lack of meaning in life, for the isolation and alienation that exist, both within society and within the Church; it also seeks to remain comfortably installed in the bosom of the Church.

It has to be said that the classical theory of charismatic Pentecostalism would see it as a protest against society, which fails to respond to the most basic needs of individuals and groups. However, all the pointers suggest that its adherents do not commit themselves to it in order to face socio-economic or political problems but, on the contrary, do so from feelings of solitude, confusion, insecurity and rootlessness. Other studies have come to more or less the same conclusions: a mentality in crisis, a strong desire for a less fallible new source of order and authority, a renewed interest in a dualistic interpretation of the world (God:Satan), a tendency to escape and a preoccupation with personal salvation. As one can see, such elements accord more with middle and upper-class requirements than with the needs of the exploited classes. On the other hand, Pentecostalism shows some of the characteristics of a formal organization: it has directors and ideology, a programme and a communications network. This is only logical, since it has a basic interest in remaining an orthodox movement within the Church in order to renew it through personal conversion. This aim is unattainable without recourse to a certain type of 'control' and direction. Its basic structure centres upon the 'prayer group'; it favours a type of warm interpersonal relationship that transcends the barriers of age, sex and race, but above all dilutes the real contradictions existing in society. Finally, Pentecostalism has an 'ideology' whose basic characteristics have been described as: rigidity, positive fatalism, rejection of the gap existing between the ideal world and the real one, and a certain personal commitment and renewing mission.

Such a description will show us that this is in fact a movement that has nothing to do with politics, yet it is precisely these characteristics that determine its political stance, even admitting its claim to be a-political. In the present structure of society any 'a-politicism' must have a direct influence on either the maintenance or the change of the *status quo*.

(*b*) From the standpoint adopted in this article there can be no 'political neutrality'. Our description of Pentecostalism leads us to think that in fact it is playing the role that some sociologists call 'attestation' (a legitimizing function), or at best 'contestation'—that is a protest that remains within the structure against which it is protesting; this has a direct political influence. Such a protest only seeks a readjustment of decayed elements of the system, not its radical change. It claims to be able to overcome social contradictions by recourse to a religious ideology. This being the case, one has to examine what social and ideological process this type of contestation can generate, and what power it shows to change the system of exploitation, or whether, on the other hand, the system is capable of controlling the social effects of such a contestation and even of favouring them. When this happens, the 'religious revival' becomes no more than the ultimate mystification practised by the ruling system, which increases its hold over other fields of social life by pushing criticism into the religious field alone. The question then arises whether this phenomenon could not in some ways be the means by which the ruling system exploits the possibilities opened up among the popular classes by the process of liberation. Whether this is true or not, what is certain is that the Pentecostalist phenomenon as it appears in Latin America today is certainly not a revolutionary religious movement.

THE PENTECOSTAL TYPE

On a deeper level, it is important to try to define the type of person who practises this mode of religiosity. In Latin America he will certainly not be found amongst the most politically aware and committed sectors of society; on the contrary, experience shows that Pentecostalism seems to be opposed to these vanguard groups. Furthermore, now that the time has come when the popular classes are beginning to display their power, and the Church in Latin America has begun to feel the weight of repression, there are many who would think that this religious phenomenon has to be placed very clearly within the overall strategy of international capitalism, which seeks to control the Churches and their most progressive elements. The degree of repression practised against the Churches that is in evidence, and the degree of control exercised over them, can only serve to heighten such a suspicion. It then becomes possible to think—and not ingenuously— that there is an actual strategy at work aimed at neutralizing the activity carried out by the Churches in favour of the poorest classes, an activity that has intolerable political effects on the system in those moments of crisis when repressive political regimes tighten their grasp in Latin America. The ideological struggle here is becoming continually more acute and it is not difficult to see the support given by power groups to reactionary religious movements that serve to hinder the exploited classes in their quest for political consciousness.

THEOLOGICAL JUDGMENT

To finish, I should like to make some observations from the theological standpoint. One of the central theological tenets of the charismatic Pentecostal movement is 'the gift of the Spirit'. When we look at the New Testament, we see that the Spirit is linked to the messianism of Jesus, that is to the meaning and import that he stamped on his life. Pentecost not only enables us to understand the connexion between his death and resurrection, but above all shows how the Pasch, identified with his historical struggle, is an effective source of liberation for us. The Ascension opens up the type of hope in which the only credible witness of the resurrected Christ will be action and proclamation of our discipleship; the Spirit was not given to dispense the disciples from their historical responsibility, but precisely to encourage and direct their actions along the same lines as their master's commitment. The presence of the Lord, paradoxically represented as 'absence', directs the Church to fulfil its central commitment—to work for the coming of justice. In this way the task for believers is to be found in the specific challenge of making the coming of the Kingdom a reality, and the Kingdom is nothing other than God's justice expressed as brotherhood between men.

By virtue of the Spirit the Church is witness to the presence of free men in a permanent struggle for their liberation. Unless it serves to awaken a new consciousness of freedom among the oppressed, all the Church's action is mere manipulation of appearances, failing to move the poor to generate more human historical forms of existence. If the central experience of the Gospel is Christ in his paschal mystery, its foremost expression is precisely the uprising of the people advancing creatively towards full liberation. The free people, the new people of God, are the fruit of the death and resurrection of Jesus Christ and the new creation of the Spirit.

The oppressed can neither believe in nor confess Jesus Christ, nor can they respond freely to him, except in so far as they succeed in freeing themselves from all oppression. They cannot be witnesses to the Spirit who liberates and transforms, except in so far as they struggle together to win a new order of justice.

The fact is that the masses of the people in the present state of the oppressed countries live in an unjust society determined by an economic base that generates violent social relationships. The form or organization of its political power, its complex juridical apparatus, and particularly its repressive ideological structures, all radically affect the process of the liberation of the people. And yet, according to the biblical tradition, we can be certain that only a people that takes stock of its own autonomy as an historical agent for transformation, can be witness to the effectiveness of redemption in Jesus Christ permanently projected and vitalized by his Spirit. The tradition of the poor is at the very root of the historical task of building a new society and a new man.

The Spirit demonstrates that true liberty is outside the law, particularly when this is identified with a legal system imposed by the interests of a ruling clique. The new meaning of Christian liberty is love, which is nothing other than liberty shared in activity aimed at transforming both society and nature.

All the evangelizing activity of the Churches is destined to clarify the voice of the Spirit calling 'Abba' from the depths of the collective will of the oppressed, as an historical claim and a radical desire for brotherhood to be brought about. If it is not directed in this way, the activity of the Churches is in vain. This is basically because evangelization is a form of freedom in action rather than a pedagogy and its fruit is precisely the emancipation of all forms of alienated consciousness, especially those imposed by an oppressive system.

Unless this general direction can be taken in the 'religious experience' of Pentecostalism, however much the biblical terms of the Christian experience are applied to it, it will remain no more than this: than a 'religious experience', and perhaps a cultural and psychological one, and this is precisely the sort of religion that favours the new repressive forms of government which today more than ever are calling themselves 'Christian'.

St Paul presents the Spirit of Christ as 'the force' behind freedom. It is then the force that drives the oppressed and changes them into the historical subject through whom God is continually redeeming history. It is just these, 'the least of the brethren', in whom the 'force' of the Spirit is made plain, with its historical power to 'make all things new'.

CONCLUSION

In so far as Pentecostalism ignores the struggle for liberation, its activity will be confined within the boundaries of immediate paternalistic concerns. It is stuck in individual spiritual renewal and in an immediate relationship with the absolute, denying historical mediations, and this makes it difficult to see how it can reject the criticism of religion as 'the opium of the people'.

Pentecostalism has not revived the old tension between charism and institution, but on the contrary seems to bring the two closer together. Once more, the official representatives of the Church are sacralizing the abandonment of the struggle. Faced with the immense problems of the impoverished majorities, the Church prefers to embrace and favour everything that assures longevity, the illusion of communion and the chimaera of a freedom that has not in fact been won. The Church is this way is content to rise from the ashes of the hope of the poor.

The Spirit of Christ still lives in 'the least of the brethren'; they are still crying, to the Churches and to the ruling system, God's protest against a society built on the blood of the innocent. Our life in the Spirit will be played out and resolved in the heart of the struggle for liberation; this implies a work of conversion in solidarity with our brothers who are suffering persecution. Freedom is the charism of charisms and this can now be seen at work in the task of the poor winning their own liberation. This means that the fruit of the Spirit is freedom and that this can only be obtained through taking part—a heroic part if needs be—in the revolutionary struggle. The Churches can be sure of one thing: they will not make a mistake if they listen to the voice of the Spirit in 'the least of the brethren'.

Translated by Paul Buons

Bibliography

J. Fichter, *The Catholic Cult of the Paraclete* (New York, 1975).

D. Gelpi, *Pentecostalism: A Theological Viewpoint* (New York, 1971).

J. Chabert, 'La hiérarchie catholique et le renouveau charismatique', in *Lumière et Vie* XXV (1975), pp. 22–3.

J. Séguy, 'Situation socio-historique du Pentécostisme', in *ibid.*, pp. 33–59.

J. Thompson, 'La participation catholique dans le mouvement du renouveau charismatique', in *Social Compass* XXI (1974), pp. 325–44.

C. Lalive d'Apinay, *Religion, dynamique sociale et dépendance* (Paris, 1975).

R. Vidales and T. Kudo, *Práctica religiosa y proyecto histórico* (Lima, 1976).

Ladislaus Boros

Discernment of the Spirit

'CHARISM' in Christian life is the grace given to one individual and to no other. This grace cannot be ordained in advance by the official organs of the Church and is not administered through the sacraments; it may be bestowed anywhere and therefore may be rediscovered anywhere. The bestowal of charisms established fruitful unrest in the Church so that through the direct effect of the Holy Spirit in the Church the individual himself could find the right form, mode and place for his personal sanctity.

The charismatic and underivable aspect is essential to the Church for God has never retired, as it were, in favour of the official ecclesial administration. Nor has he abdicated in favour of the guidance of the Holy Spirit given to the higher and highest instances of the Church. God himself is the Spirit blowing where he listeth; and he blows alike on children and idiots, the poor and simple, and theologians of all kinds.

There have always been non-official charismatics in the Church who have exercised the cure of souls: the prophets of the Didache, the monastic pneumatics of the early Greek Church, and Benedict and Francis, who were not priests. Wherever a charismatic of this type lives and works within a church context, he should not encounter unnecessary obstacles. No one in the Christian life should forget Paul's warning of Satan's ability to appear in the guise of an angel of light (2 Cor. 11:14). A Christian should not give immediate credence to even the most sacred phenomena. Ignatius of Loyola in his *Spiritual Exercises*[1] is very emphatic about that: 'It is characteristic of the angel of wickedness who transforms himself into an angel of light to appear with a pious spirit but eventually to reveal his real self. In other words: he professes first of all good and holy sentiments appropriate to so right-eous a soul but then tries to reach his own objectives by drawing the soul into his own deception and perversion'. Piety, upright striving for what is good and for good opinion are therefore insufficient in our world in which extreme cunning is widely practised. We have to discern the various spirits.

John warns us very strongly: '. . . do not believe every spirit but test the spirits to see whether they are of God' (1 John 4:13). And Paul is perhaps even more emphatic when he says: 'Do not quench the Spirit . . . but test everything; hold fast what is good' (1 Thess. 5:19.21). The individual, charismatic life of the Christian in the world has to be lived between these two: 'Do not quench the Spirit' and 'do not believe every spirit'.

Major Christian thinkers have paid much attention to the problem of discerning the spirits. Their thoughts on the subject are to be found in excellent monographs.[2] I should like to concentrate on the high-point of these reflections: on the rules for the discernment of spirits which Ignatius gave us in his *Exercises*. Ignatius in doing that was treading a dangerous path. I shall try here to follow up his exploration of the subject.[3]

The rules for the discernment of spirits begin with an apparently harmless statement. Every really great and creative perception seems at first ridiculously simple:

OPPOSITE EFFECTS OF DIFFERENT SPIRITS

The spirits work differently in people according to whether they are in a state of sin or a state of grace. That must be so. God appears quite differently to the man who continually rejects him than to one who is always trying to make more room for God in his life. The first two rules are so clear that one can almost completely dispense with commentary: 'The evil one usually parades pleasures before the eyes of those who go from one grave sin to another, and he does so by evoking images of sensual delight and pleasure, in order to keep them in their bonds and sin, and to allow them to increase them. The good spirit behaves in a diametrically opposed way with such creatures. He stirs them and prods their conscience through the inner voice of reason'. 'The proce-dure of the spirits among those who are really aware and advance from good to better in the service of the Lord God is opposed to that de-scribed in the first rule. For now it is characteristic of the evil spirit to sear the soul, speaking in sadness and setting up obstacles by upsetting the soul on false grounds, so that it does not stride ahead. And it is characteristic of the good Spirit to give courage and strength, comfort, tears, assurance and quiet, by making everything easy and removing all obstacles, so that one can do better.

Ignatius summarized these two rules thus: 'Among those who advance from the good to the better, the good angel stirs the soul sweetly, softly and mildly like a drop of water entering a sponge. Those however who proceed from the bad to the worse are stirred in the opposite way by spirits of evil. The cause of these things is that the soul is constituted as, or in opposition to, these spirits. If it is contrary, then they enter in with a great noise and clatter. If it is like, then the spirit quietly enters in as if through an open door to his own house'.

For Ignatius of Loyola, then, neither peace, joy, consolation, quiet, tenderness or gentleness nor their contraries (upset, sadness, unrest, noise, harshness and fierceness) are lacking in deception, whether one is under the influence of a good or an evil spirit. The different effects can be decided only in terms of the overall condition of the soul. But that state of soul in its turn is judged by Ignatius according to the inner dynamics of one's life: according to one's progress (either from the good to the better, or from the bad to the worse). This is extremely important. The spirits, whether good or bad, can only 'do something' to or with people in whose lives something is happening.

The surest protection against any influence of spirits is to be an ordinary average kind of person. Those whose awareness is hardly distinct from their general social world; those who want to be like others; those whose souls are deeply stirred neither by evil nor by good, who do good or evil only because they have nothing else to do; those whose heads are so chaotic that angel or devil would find it difficult to awaken them from passivity, so that they live their awareness with a clarity in which a real decision would be possible—such people are no arena for the spirits. Ignatius did not write his rules for discerning spirits for people of that kind.

The knowledge that spirits can only affect those to whom something is happening prompts us to consider how a spirit can influence men anyway. Here Ignatius would most probably say that a created spirit can only enter an already flowing stream of thoughts, considerations, feelings and sensations.[4] Neither devils nor angels have a power over us that would enable them to touch the core of our being. Their presence can only latch on to the external traces of our inward reality. In the very inwardness of our being we are 'only ourselves', untouchable and closed to manipulation. There we are alone with God. Anyone leading a self-critical and cultivated life is aware of such direct effects of the spirits.

We experience it every day. We might try one day to do something good and just. Perhaps we want to rouse someone from a confused spiritual condition and we succeed. Everything we do fits together and the result is there in all its beauty and grace and we experience a feeling of humble thankfulness. Another time it just doesn't work. We are disturbed by outward circumstances or through our own inner weakness. We do not find the right word at the right moment. We cannot manage that additional something that would give what we have said and done the power of witness. In the end something small and deceptive is produced. Ignatius was much better at describing this experience: 'We must submit our inspirations and thoughts to a strict and attentive examination. Their beginning, progress and end must all be carefully considered. Are all these good? It is, then, our good angel that inspired them. On the other hand, is there anything intrinsically bad, anything that leads us away from good, or that urges us to something below what we had chosen; anything that fatigues the soul, casts it into anguish and trouble, makes it lose the peace, the repose, the serenity which it enjoyed? If we discover on reflection that such is the case, it is an evident sign that the inspiration comes from the spirit of darkness, and that it conceals some snare he is laying for us'.

But let us return to our original point: the spirits can affect our lives only indirectly, by influencing the operations of the soul. Only God can directly affect the soul. This brings us to the very core of the rules for discerning spirits.

THE DIRECTNESS OF GOD

We must be clear about what Ignatius meant by the directness of God. The relevant texts are as follows: 'When a natural cause of consolation has preceded, who has sent it? Perhaps our good angel, perhaps the bad.' 'The Creator alone can penetrate his creature, raise him, change him, enkindle in him the fire of his love. Hence, when nothing has been presented to the senses, the intellect, the will of a nature to cause joy, and yet the soul is consoled all at once without antecedent cause, then it is God that acts upon it'. And finally, with great assurance and exactitude: 'It is God who visits the soul when no natural cause has led to the consolation with which it is suddenly filled'. Accordingly the soul is then wholly delivered up to God.

How are we to understand this directness of God? Ignatius says that God appears as consolation. He means of course that condition in which the soul, consciously or unconsciously, strives towards God. For only then can it experience God as consolation. In the state of orientation to God, a man follows his usual pursuits, works, talks to others, goes out into nature, cares for his family and friends. Suddenly he finds light in doing all that. The air is clearer, colours are brighter, his heart beats more confidently and he is quite open. With all his fragility he feels that he is taken up into the Quite-other. Ignatius does not scruple to say that that means God.

Ignatius speaks in this context of a divine movement of the soul that assuredly emanates from God. This is a primary evidence of the Divine within a specific consolation. Such an occurrence must of necessity be underivable. God can be directly experienced only through God himself. The first and indeed sole characteristic of direct consolation through God is accordingly the non-objective nature of the event; in other words, that it was not brought about by any created reality in the proper sense. Here it seems appropriate to refer to the metaphysical structure of human knowledge.[5]

Man perceives that which is actual, bounded, endowed with content. At the same time, however, he strives beyond all that towards the region of the boundless. The twofold movement of the Spirit is present in every cognition. Man can only recognize that which is bounded in that he is drawn by that which is boundless. That which is present in the human soul as a consciously effected cognition is never more than the actual nature as content of the circumscribed, or that which the cognitive faculty elicits from it. The uncircumscribed dynamics on the other hand is unconscious, incomplete, unthematic; even though it is present in every cognition (as presupposition, condition and inward rule), being the most profound ground of all knowledge. It is none other than the drawing power of God in the human spirit. This attraction opens man up so that he thrusts beyond himself and is forever dissatisfied with what he has already achieved. Accordingly the attraction is experienced in the soul only in a 'negative' form. Man experiences his own dissatisfaction with the circumscribed; he knows that he is essentially disillusioned with everything that he has accomplished to date. Now we have, if only in preliminary form, all the elements we need in order to answer the question of what the Ignatian groundless consolation may be, and why it is the most assured sign of God's presence in the soul.

The following can happen through the grace of God: God so to speak 'intensifies' his attraction and one consciously experiences the fact that he was always present with us; that we have conceived him along with every cognition without expressly experiencing him. Such an event then appears 'groundless' and is in fact derivable from nothing possessed of content; from nothing that is to be experienced otherwise. The attraction of God is the ground of all cognitions; it is the very essence of grounding: something that is no longer derivable from any other ground. Hence the 'groundlessness' of a consolation (which does not necessarily mean its 'suddenness') is the proper and sure indication that it is God himself who is consoling us.

There is something important that we must remember in this context. The experienced nearness of God which affects the human consciousness as 'groundless consolation' is indeed 'consolation'. Comfort is not a mere accompaniment of the experience of the closeness of God. Here (and only here) it is certainly true that peace, joy, rest and felicity are wholly trustworthy signs of the presence of God. When essential, groundless happiness overcomes one, that is the conscious experience of what one always was as a Christian. Ignatius leaves no room for doubt here: God is boundless happiness and life with him is felicity. To experience this happiness and radiate it in the world is the specific duty of a Christian life. The Christian's duty is to be happy.[6]

Hence we are now able to say how man (who, if he has bound himself wholly to God, is willing to advance from the good to the better) can discover what God requires of him in his particular life-situation. He should search for happiness; everything else will happen of itself. God's will is to be found in the adventure of consolation.

THE ADVENTURE OF CONSOLATION

Unfortunately there is no space here to enter into many aspects of the Ignatian discernment of spirits. I shall draw attention only to those that seem most important, offering some indications of those that can be of assistance in certain situations.

'During times of desolation, the bad spirit makes us feel his influence. By following his inspirations we cannot arrive at any good or useful decision; we must, therefore, beware at such times of reconsidering or making any innovation whatsoever in what relates to our resolutions or choice of a state of life; but we must persevere in what we have decided on in the day or hour of consolation, and consequently under the influence of the good spirit'.

Or again: 'Under the pressure of desolation the following are the thoughts which should sustain us: Divine grace remains to us although it may have ceased to be sensible; although the first ardour of our charity is no longer felt, we still have all that is requisite for doing good and working out our salvation'. And again: 'When consolation abounds in the heart, we must consider the conduct to be observed in time of trial; and to sustain the shock, we must provide in good time a supply of courage and vigorous resolution'. Then there is the fundamental and well-proven observation: 'Satan, with his weak but obstainate character, may be compared, when he attacks us, to a woman daring to contend with her husband. Let her husband oppose her firmly, she soon lays aside her warlike mood, and quickly leaves the field to him; on the contrary, let her see in him any timidity or inclination to fly or give way, she becomes audacious, insolent, cruel as a fury. So when Satan sees the soldier of Jesus Christ, his heart imperturbable, his head erect, repulsing every attack without flinching, he immediately loses courage; but if he perceives him trembling at the first shock and ready to ask quarter, he immediately attacks him with a rage, a fury, a ferocity which is unexampled among wild beasts enraged against their prey: obstinate in his infernal malice, he only seeks and breathes our ruin'. And then: 'When we have discovered the infernal serpent . . . it is very useful to go over again in spirit the way by which the tempter led us, to take to pieces the plot he had so cleverly laid . . . the study of his odious manoeuvres will render us more capable of escaping them for the future'.

These remarks reveal a man whose soul was fired by God and who, strong against the wiles of the world, was able with patience, clarity, objectivity and even a certain degree of humour (almost always a sign of sincerity) to translate his mystical experience into actual life terms for the inspiration of others.

However important the foregoing indications may be, they are not so significant as the fundamental insight: if a human life is stirred by the thrust of grace; if it is in accord with God and his angels, then happiness is a sure sign that a concrete decision will lead in the right direction. This is the foundation of the discovery of the actual will of God. By this Ignatius seems to say: you have made a decision in your life in favour of order. You will no longer tarry in this condition but advance from this good to a better state. The question is now how you are to recognize what is better in your life. Often you will be put in a situation in which you no longer know what is the right thing to do, let alone what might be the better course. But if you remain true to your fundamental inclination, then there is a strait and narrow way for you. Always try to face your future subsidiary decisions with your experience of happiness. But remain honest and sincere. If you see that a decision makes you happier in the whole of your Christian existence, then make it and take the direction prescribed by your happiness. God is leading you, either himself or through his good angel.

But the question is what Ignatius means by happiness or, as he puts it, 'consolation'. From his various exercises and rules we can draw up a list of 'consolations': interior peace, spiritual joy, ignition of the soul, tears at the suffering of Christ, at one's own sins and at those of others; things that contribute directly to the laud and honour of God, tenderness, resolution, gentleness, raising up of the spirit, inward clarity. And in happiness, according to Ignatius, we also find repentance, sympathy with Christ and selfless self-sacrifice. Ignatius is not concerned with the superficial in any way: with thoughtless merriment or fleeting pleasures. He is concerned with genuine happiness, with what enlarges the soul and enables it to breathe in the elements of purity, love and security. Hence the man who is looking for God should slowly feel his way into his divinely willed existence; into his specific form of holiness in the world which can be fulfilled by no other person.

With every (even if perhaps only tentative) step he approaches that reality which accords with every man who is graced, able to support life in this world and securely rooted in God; in fact he approaches that condition of man which God conceived when he made man this man.[7]

That happiness of which Ignatius speaks here can accompany sharp pain, earthly sorrow and temporal loss. It can exist in the midst of the greatest difficulties of everyday life, in weariness and in dryness of spirit, in the terrible darkness of existential need, and even in the state of godforsakenness. Essentially it is nothing other than a quiet knowledge that in the ultimate ground of his existence man is secure and safe in the love of God. There is nothing spurious about it and nothing superficial. It is the openness of the soul to God; the experience that being is essentially good and that life is worth living; that nothing that is not heaven can penetrate the profundity of our existence. It is with this feeling of ultimate security in God that a Christian must face his individual decisions. If a decision that is good in itself does not nourish this feeling of security in God, then it is best to avoid it and look for other possible courses. This search must be undertaken in a peaceful and lucid state of equanimity. But the last word in genuinely Christian decisions (that is, those which touch upon our eternal salvation) should be pronounced by happiness, our experience of security in God. The ultimate itself is unpredictable.

I have tried here to present some of the aspects of the Ignation 'discernment of spirits'. I follow him in summarizing a movement of spiritual history which is unfortunately far too often neglected. It might be said that my presentation offers little help in the practical tasks of life. Perhaps that is the case. But if we make our decisions on the basis of such fundamental experiences we shall influence human history more than we suspect. The most powerful impulses are born of such experiences. In such instances the spiritual director should not forget Ignatius' advice that he should allow the Christian to 'communicate directly with his Creator'.

Translated by John Maxwell

Notes

1. The original text of the Exercises is cited here according to my own translation.

2. Especially interesting material on the patristic *Discretio spirituum* is to be found in A. Chellet, 'Discernement des esprits' in *Dictionnaire de Théologie catholique*, IV (Paris, 1911), cols. 1375-91.

3. See, especially on the historical implications: H. Rahner, ' "Werdet kundige Geldwechsler". Zur Geschichte der Lehre des heiligen Ignatius von Loyola von der Unterscheidung der Geister', in F. Wulf, *Ignatius von Loyola. Seine geistige Gestalt und sein Vermächtnis* (Würzburg, 1966), pp. 301–41. See also: Fridolin Marxer, *Die inneren geistlichen Sinne. Ein Beitrag zur Deutung ignatianischer Mystik* (Freiburg, 1963), esp. pp. 119–32.

4. There are remarkable points of agreement between the teaching of Ignatius of Loyola and that of Origen. See in this regard, Hans Urs von Balthaser, *Origenes. Geist und Feuer. Ein Aufbau aus seinen Schriften* (Salzburg & Leipzig, 1938), esp. pp. 330–41.

5. On this entire aspect, see J. Maréchal, *Le point de départ de la métaphysique* (Louvain & Paris, 1922-6), esp, fasc. 5: 'Le thomisme devant la philosophie critique'. Maréchal died in Louvain in 1944 before he had completed his work (fasc. 6 was to treat contemporary theories of knowledge). His influence can be traced in neo-scholastic philosophy today and is apparent in many publications.

6. See in this respect Teilhard de Chardin, *Le Milieu Divin: An Essay on the Interior Life* (London & New York, 1960).

7. In my book *Im Leben Gott Erfahren* (Olten, second ed., 1976; Eng. trans.: *Meeting God in Man*, London & New York, 1967), I have tried to show the variety of existential experience of God. We have no right to forbid any specific way of access to God.

Christian Duquoc

Charism as the Social Expression of the Unpredictable Nature of Grace

ON 27 January 1977, the Congregation for the Doctrine of Faith published a document on 'the question of the admission of women to the sacerdotal ministry'. It clearly raises the problem of the relation of the gratuitous nature of the charisms to their institutional control. The text steers clear of any pejorative judgment of the condition of women and their inability to assume ecclesial and spiritual responsibilities in a fruitful way. The authors of the declaration even go out of their way to show how strongly the church of Rome supports the equality of rights between man and woman and refer to the struggle for women's liberation. Consequently the exclusion of woman from the sacerdotal ministry is not the effect of a discrimination based on considerations of a socio-psychological nature: one cannot therefore base the argument for the refusal of access to the sacerdotal ministry on the ground of the 'specific nature' of woman.

   If this inability of a woman to enter the priestly ministry does not spring from her nature, nor from her condition, nor from psychological factors, it can only derive from a decision based on another free decision which belongs to the order of grace. It is this direction which the declaration takes: Jesus, who showed such an astonishing freedom in his attitude towards social assumptions, did not choose any women as apostles but only men. This choice would not have such definitive implications as the Church of Rome has attributed to him if in other ways Jesus had shown himself a prisoner of contemporary prejudice on other important points. As the text recognizes in all honesty, it would no doubt be impossible for us to draw such a rigid conclusion from

Jesus' silence and the mere fact of his choosing only men for the apostolate if we were not faced with a constant tradition of the Church of Rome and the Orthodox Church. But once we accept that such a unanimous tradition cannot err in its interpretation of Scripture, one has to conclude that this silence and this choice of Jesus take on an importance for the future of the Church which scientific exegesis by itself cannot ignore. From its own point of view the Church of Rome maintains that it has no power whatever to abrogate a decision which goes back to Jesus himself. It can only accept it in all humility and, far from wanting women to feel inferior it makes every effort to show that this decision compels it to stress that their personality cannot be reduced to the masculine model, and that real Christian dignity does not lie in the exercise of ministries but in living according to the Gospel. There is no such thing as a right to charisms, but there are demands from the community that one should live according to the requirements of the Gospel. In his sovereign freedom, the Spirit chooses who shall be endowed with the charism required for the life of the Church.

I have recalled the content of this document because it highlights the ambiguous way in which the Church's administration handles grace. There is, indeed, no decisive argument whatsoever to justify the preferential and exclusive choice of males for the exercise of the sacerdotal ministry. This priesthood is a charism given for the sake of the community. I stress the fact that it is a charism because it is not based on any natural, psychological authority which is inherent in the male but on a gratuitous decision: i.e., it is not inherently imposed. It is only when the decision is assumed to be irrevocable that arguments are put forth to justify it. As today the movements for women's liberation have become powerful, the text puts forward the traditional view as a positive element of this liberation. In spite of the precautions the ambiguity persists. The decision sets up an order, a hierarchy, which, because of its divine origin, it becomes sociologically difficult to explain otherwise than as natural. In fact, to exclude women from the sacerdotal ministry means, in the traditional organization of the Church of Rome which links this ministry with the magisterium and government, excluding them from every stage of decision-taking and treating them as minors. In brief, the gratuitous decision, which has no natural basis, organizes the men-women relationship on a hierarchical model in which the women are objects of this decision-taking, never the active participants. Thus the charism, in this case, reinforces the existing order of the subjection of woman, and this subjection is often deemed to be a part of the natural order. It provides a divine guarantee for what is taking place on a majority basis.

In order to bring out the paradoxical nature of the legislation or institutionalization of the charism or grace, let us imagine that it is decided to give force of law to the parable about the 'labourers of the eleventh hour' (Mt 20:1–16). This would lead to a social order in total contradiction with justice, and the phrase: 'Am I not allowed to do what I choose with what belongs to me? (Mt 20:15) would become the justification of exploitation by him who, because of his economically stronger situation, has the money and imposes the terms of the contract on him who only can dispose of his labour. Thus the real point of the parable, which is to show that in God's dealings with man 'value' and 'gift' cannot be equated, would reinforce a socially repulsive procedure by legalizing it. Is it then not a contradiction to turn what is essentially free into a legal way of ordering society? Can charisms and grace be subjected to legislation? Is it not undertaking the impossible to want to manage God's gifts through institutional management, which is what the Churches and particularly the Church of Rome are doing? It is this kind of problem which Leszek Kolakowski has examined in a study entitled: 'Chrétiens sans Eglise. La Conscience et le lien confessionel au XVIIᵉ siècle' (Christians without church. The religious consciousness and the confessional bond in the XVIIth century) (Paris, 1969). Before I deal with the meaning for the Church of the tension this author has brought to light, I want to concentrate on one element of the author's thesis. This will then allow me to spell out in a different language the problems which underlie the position taken up by the Congregation for the Faith on the question of admitting women to the sacerdotal ministry.

KOLAKOWSKI'S THESIS: GRACE MEANS ABSENCE OF ORDER

Kolakowski does not set up an abstract thesis which he then tries to prove. In a scholarly study he found that the non-denominational (non-confessional) and mystical movements of the XVIIth century, whether Protestant or Catholic, showed an allergy to the institutional nature of the traditional churches. This allergy was not a transitory mood or some particular kind of anarchy: the author thought it was something inherent in the very dynamics of Christianity. This Christianity implies a contradiction in its very structure because it has a fundamental unifying concept and combines it with the concept of grace which is seen as having nothing to do with order. I will deal very briefly with the way in which he tries to prove his statement.

The God of the New Testament is an innovator when compared with the God of the Old Testament. Jesus' God is not a legislator but a father. He forgives without asking for compensation; He forgives because He loves the human beings who are his children. In return, human beings cling to him, not in order to escape some punishment inflicted by a judge, but because he is their father. Thus the religion based on the law is replaced by the religion based on the irrational bond of a family. This substitution of a legal contract by a bond of affection is the characteristic feature of the Christian view of the world. No doubt, in theory or theologically one can reconcile the images of judge, legislator and father, but in practice, i.e., in religious experience, this proves impossible because these images induce attitudes that are too far opposed. It is an illusion to want to live up to them all. One obeys the commandments either out of fear or because of unselfish love. Only the latter attitude corresponds to the 'novelty' of Christianity.

Obedience motivated by disinterested love makes one realize that, since love implies duty, duty as such becomes unnecessary in the relation between man and God. 'Love, and do what you want', said St Augustine. In the end it is impossible for the freedom, born of grace, to co-exist in a lasting way with the order of the law. According to Kolakowski grace is not a supplement to the law but negates it since it reverses the rational order. Grace is arbitrary on principle and has no connexion with justice.

Kolakowski has no hesitation in saying that no theology has managed to give a satisfactory explanation of the law and grace in historical Christianity. On the one hand one draws attention to the mystery of divine decisions, or to some predestination, or to some vocation, wholly unrelated to any merit or value whatever. On the other hand, the Church is an historical institution and has to give itself a right and laws in order to survive. In charge of maintaining an order and traditions, it is not less loud in proclaiming the gratuitousness of the Gospel for all that. It is weighed down under the burden of the gospels because, says Kolakowski, although the Church has tried in many ways to make them inaccessible to the people it has not been able to prevent that from the most simple Christians to the most learned ones there is an awareness of a clash between the ecclesial or moral order and the irrationality of grace and the gifts of the Spirit.

As a matter of fact, the Spirit has nowhere stipulated that he would only manifest himself through the medium of ecclesial institutions or the sacraments. No one has ever dared call into question the fact that he is master of his own gifts or even that he can give himself to the pagans, as evidenced by an event related in the Acts of the Apostles (Acts 10:44-8). No one has ever denied that the Spirit can have a genuine relationship with a believer without the intervention and authorization of some ecclesiastical body. But what then is the point of having ecclesiastical criteria in order to authenticate the gifts? And yet, who can tell whether a particular communication from God is really a contact with God or the madness of pride? How can we extricate ourselves from the dilemma? If the Church judges the matter as the final court of appeal, it judges God, and whether one likes it or not, the law rules grace. But if everyone decides for himself whether the divine communication is genuine and if the sole criterion of divine authenticity is the experience of the person who perceives the voice of the Spirit in his heart, there is no longer any point in having a Church at all. And so Kolakowski is not afraid of putting the Christian paradox in blunt terms: the Church administers or manipulates grace by integrating it into the law, which means: by denying it. When, therefore, the Church imposes what must be done or judges what has to be done, it suppresses the irrationality, the gratuitousness and the freedom of grace. The Church pretends to distribute grace equally, but that is to deny grace which, by its very essence, is non-just: 'The impossibility of renouncing belief in grace and the impossibility of existing in any other way than by denying this belief is a specific feature of the Church'.

Kolakowski sees in this contradiction the matrix of the spiritual movements and the various kinds of modernism which continually spring up in the Churches. These phenomena are not pathological, but natural. Inspired by the gospel of grace, condemned by the legalism of the institution, these movements are groping for new forms of expression. These forms obey a desire which lies concealed in the inner contradictory nature of the Churches seen as the rational incarnation of the 'irrational radiation of grace'.

Hence, the heresies born of the gratuitousness of grace are as it were the second nature of the Church. And in this sense the New Testament is the book of heresies. There arise, indeed, constantly believers in the Church for whom the law cannot positively achieve freedom, but only limit it. Grace is the positive freedom of God; it is in some way an irrational spontaneity which can only be determined by his good will. This is what the dogma of predestination tried to express. The order of the law and the gratuitousness of grace (or the absence of order) can only be combined by mutual limitation or negation. This kind of combination is clearly impossible. The Church constantly limps between two contradictory poles. It manipulates opposite realities. If movements spring up within the Church which are charismatic or mystical or not interested in the confessional bond, it is because they find their inspiration in that Church and at the same time their rejection. According to Kolakowski, the reason for this situation lies in the nature of the

Church which is the habitat of a contradiction between a grace which by definition encourages the absence of order and a law which by wanting to embody this grace, denies it.

CHARISM: GRATUITOUSNESS AND COMMUNITY

Kolakowski's presentation of the opposition between grace and the ecclesial institution is based on the analysis of historical movements. It also relies on data from the New Testament. 'This wind blows where it wills, and you hear the sound of it, but you do not know whence it comes or whither it goes; so it is with every one who is born of the Spirit' (Jn 3:8). It is difficult to think of a text that is more anti-institutional. Yet, in spite of this historical and biblical support, I wonder how valid the justification of this bi-partite combination of grace and institution is, which makes us think of the reality of the Church in terms of a dilemma. It seems to me that a dilemma is not the best way of expressing as one unit the jointing of grace or the Spirit and the ecclesial institution. Hypothetically the management of administration of a contradictory reality, the Church, aims at keeping together in a kind of living organism the twofold dominance of gratuitousness with its personal and collective distribution on the one hand, and its social or institutional expression on the other. In his presentation Kolakowski forgets that it is a function of the ecclesial institution actively to bring to light the gratuitous and in a way unpredictable nature of its own origin and survival. There is a witness to this dynamism where there is an interchange between the unpredictable or the happening and the institutional, and this witness is the charism. The charism is the social or institutional form which is assumed by the gratuitousness of grace. The ecclesial institution is not an organization which is planned for taking on functionaries with rigorously defined jobs.

The Church is not an institution devoting itself first of all to organizing its survival by creating a juridical and legislative constitution. It is not the purpose of its social organization to deny what permanently remains its present origin, namely, God's grace or good will, evidenced in the gift of the Spirit. I do not dispute the fact that Kolakowski's historical analyses point in a direction which leads to the pattern of a dilemma; what I do dispute is that this pattern is so dominant that it excludes any vital connection between the ecclesial institution and what is at the same time the origin and *raison d'être* of this institution, namely, grace, or the Spirit. The sign of this intended vital connection seems to me to be the charism.

What I mean is that the ecclesial institution integrates the possibility of the unpredictable, at least in its origin. Since the function of the charisms is social, serving the ends of the community, the charisms bear witness at the core of the institution to the fact that it is necessary for its very survival not to lock itself up in a legal order or a rationally planned organization. The charism shows that the responsibilities within the institution and for the ends of the community do not exclusively depend on juridicial or legally definable processes. It is inherent in the life of the Church as an institution that, ultimately, its orientation and future cannot be decided by any juridical power.

The prevailing idea that in the Catholic Church juridical processes control and regularize the charisms is right, but only partly so or even one-sided. It would be just as correct to say that the charisms control and regularize the legal processes. It is in this sense that I include the unpredictable and the gratuitous in the institution. The charism constitutes a bridge between the happening and the institution, the gratuitous and the legal, the unpredictable and what is planned, the Spirit and the structure.

No doubt to some extent Kolakowski's thesis remains true—not only in so far as it provides historical evidence, particularly in Catholicism—but, first of all, it seems to me, in that it shows up the conflicting nature of the Church. Because of its own weight the institution leans over towards a reducing of this conflict to a matter of ill will or sin. In actual fact the conflict is tied up with the institution itself because it aims at making the freedom of grace livable at both the social and the personal levels. The juridical power, which in Catholicism has assumed a highly sophisticated clerical form, has organized itself in such a way that is can keep control of all those initiatives on which, in its view, the Church's survival and future depend. This tendency explains why so many so-called spiritual movements have been rejected in history. The unforseen (because unpredictable) ways of serving the Gospel and the community were seen by the legally organized power structure as a danger to the balance achieved so far and an adventure deemed to be sinful. So the juridical or legal processes of the Church's power structure aim at controlling any initiative which has not originated from their own decision. Even today the notions of 'mandate' or 'mission' are still only used to justify this control. These notions restrict both socially and ecclesiastically any initiative which does not fall within the scope laid down by the 'mandate'. Thus, in France, there is no other way of explaining the privileged status of Catholic Action. No doubt, in a number of cases the organization is more formal than real. Nevertheless, the organization shows that its 'authorities' are unable to accept the changes and unpredictabilities of the Church's life when it is moved by the Spirit. These terms of 'mandate' and 'mission' tend to throw out any social responsibility within the Church or the community simply because the juridical or legal hierarchy are not involved in it. It is therefore not just an accident if the spiritual movements, aimed at the community at large, have often arisen in history in opposition to the power of a legalistic hierarchy.

The dilemma Kolakowski is so fond of corresponds to a real situation: that of an ecclesiastical policy against which spiritual movements have always battled. The interests which the institution defends on the ground of the choice of its representative authorities seem to these movements too far removed from the aims which it proclaimed publicly to pursue. In order to prevent the spiritual movements from invading the domain of its decisions ecclesiastical policy tends to limit the gratuitousness of grace exclusively to matters of the inner life, thus leaving no room for the breakthrough of the Spirit at the social level. In reality this policy is contrary to the structure of the ecclesial institution since, from the start, this includes the charism as a social expression and not as a purely inner feature of the life of the faithful. The result is that, within the institution, the charism excludes the domination of the law or the organization; it defies the monopolization of social power within the Church by a caste which legitimizes its position only through legalism. The charism stresses the fact that the Spirit is not the prisoner of the inner life and it bears positive witness to his power to raise within the institution and to the advantage of its aim which is life according to the Gospel men and women for whom concern for the Kingdom of God comes first. Kolakowski's thesis about grace as absence of order and about the institutional Church as its inevitable opposite springs from the observation that an institution treating the law as privileged while proclaiming the supremacy of grace limps between anarchy (however much restricted to the inner life or the fringe) and legalism.

If, in spite of this contradiction the Church has survived and there has been no irreparable explosion it is only because ultimately there are still bridges between the one and the other, grace and the institution. The purpose of the institution is not to deny the unpredictable nature of grace nor to drive its gratuitousness back within the confines of the inner life exclusively; it is also to show these two features in history and therefore in the social body which it builds up, even at the cost of painful and constant changes. In this sense the charism is vital for a Church which is subordinated to the gratuitousness of the Gospel and means to bear witness to this through the life of the community.

These reflections on the charism as the social expression which is necessary to show in the Church's life the gratuitousness and unpredictability of the grace of the Gospel lead us to look again at the Roman text on the exclusion of women from the sacerdotal ministry. To exercise a ministry in the Church is not a right in the sense in which we speak today of the right to work. From this point of view, no particular man or woman can claim to have a right to a responsible position in the ministry. It is God who, in the Spirit and through the mediation of the community, chooses those who are destined to help the Christian community to achieve its proper object, which is to live according to the Gospel of Jesus Christ. But once this has been said, the question remains wide open. Indeed, to exclude women from access to the ministry amounts to legalizing a charism. It means making a law according to which it is decided that human beings, because of their sex, and therefore because of a natural condition, are excluded *a priori* from ever being seized by the Spirit in order to help the community through the ministry or the priesthood. Whether one likes it or not, the natural condition is itself the condition of the charism. Here it is not a case of the charism exploding the institutional but of the institutional restricting the charism. To refer to the will of Jesus when he never expressed it is not enough to justify the kind of relation put forward here between the charism and what has been instituted. All the precautions taken to make it clear that this is not a question of assuming that the male is superior to the female do not change the exclusive bending of a gratuitousness which is turned into a preference of nature. As to the explanations which point out that Jesus was a male and that therefore only males can symbolize the presidency of the Eucharist, this amounts to saying that in the ministry the natural condition is more important than the breath of the Spirit which precisely breaks down all the barriers imprisoning men and women, all created in the likeness of God.

The sacraments have developed in a strange way: starting from human symbols and based on a free act of Jesus, they were meant to express the gratuitousness and unpredictability of grace. They have become the most untouchable elements of a legal system. Far from being the source of a transforming dynamism, they are now part of an unchangeable structure. It demands uncommon energy to defend their everlastingness at the same time as their liberating nature. But this is what the Roman text wants to do by trying to show that it is to the advantage of the female condition that woman would not hold any responsible ministry in the Church. Thus the sacrament of orders is a legality which no charism will disturb. This Roman document shows the difficulty for the Catholic Church in trying to escape from the dilemma of grace or institution. Its tendency to legalize the charisms reasserts itself in spite of the efforts made since Vatican II to soften a discipline as damaging to the truth of a law as to the gratuitousness of the gift. Indeed, what I have just written about the ministry of women could also be applied with a few modifications to the lasting character of the sacrament of orders or of the law of celibacy. Signifying the unpredictable, the charism is an instrument of flexibility in the institution. By throwing it out, the institution creates tensions which end up in ruptures.

If these reflections on a Roman document and a work of history need any conclusion, I would say this: it seems to me that the charisms are at the core of the ecclesial institution as a form of gratuitousness and unpredictability which checks and regularizes the phenomenon of legalization and hierarchization. This phenomenon appears almost instinctively in all forms of religion and is the more damaging to Christianity as it contradicts the proclamation made by the highest officials of the Church. The Roman text discussed here shows that contradiction: it legalizes the charism of the ministry whilst showing that this, far from subjecting women, works for their liberation. Whatever the Church may do, it can only preach this liberation, otherwise it would deny its origin.

Translated by Theo Weston

PART II

Bulletins

Paul Abela

Celebrating and then Practising the Eucharist

AMONGST the reasons that seem to explain the difficulty of dialogue between the Church and the World, the experience gained over thirty years of actively engaged life suggests that there are two principal ones:

The essence of the faith is lived and judged in terms of brotherly love.[1] Sacramental practice and a large part of prayer belong to the order of means: they are a source to which one can return, a means of recycling in order to prepare for action. If, as I believe, religion goes beyond the bounds of morality and praxis in its deepest life and its final ontological aim, it is nevertheless carried out in praxis and will be judged on its praxis.[2]

An inadequate language leads to tragic misunderstanding. This stems from the clumsiness, stiffness and inertia of the Church; but this crisis of language also shows up the underlying theology it reflects: too often it must surely be imputed to laziness, pretentiousness and decay hiding under cover of fidelity to the letter. Such a situation requires a new effort of attentiveness and greater readiness to use the imagination and boldness required by the situation, or, if one is not capable of this, one has to give in (because not everyone is blessed with the creative readiness required).[3]

WORDS AND THINGS

When I took part about ten years ago with several other lay people from France in one of the sub-commissions for translating and adapting the four post-conciliar eucharistic prayers, there were several of us who felt the weakness of some traditional language; certain words and expressions still used in the liturgy and catechesis have become meaningless for our contemporaries. Such words would be: expiation, redemption, sacrificed victim, Lamb of God, this is my Body, God is holy, the kingdom, the power and the glory, and so on. We were not able to win the day then but the unease we felt still remains and these words, which form the heart of liturgical texts, still stick in our throats.

One has to recognize that such expressions, which have been considerably enriched through centuries of usage, have a real, deep and respectable meaning in every sense for those who live deeply what they express, but for lay people, impregnated as they are with secular language, their necessarily more modest initiation into such words and expressions is not enough to prevent their meaning from slipping, fading and even disappearing. The overall impression they leave is too vague, too devoid of significance, in the long run boring and even misleading and alienating. The esoteric nature of this language then becomes a means of enslavement (abuse of hierarchical pressure on both knowledge and action); a source of alienation (misunderstanding of the essential meaning); of pharisaism or of disaffection. If this language requires too long an initiation to be appreciated, it is élitist and can then not suit the mass of believers or claim to be vital (otherwise it would be immoral). An expression suited to every man, to the man in the street, and therefore necessarily to the 'poor' must go straight to the heart of the matter, speak to the heart of those who are willing to listen and not offer too easy a way open to escapism. Fernando Belo in his *Lecture matérialiste de L'Evangile de Marc* has recently denounced the stress that has for too long been placed on the sacred, the pure and the impure, the priestly and the mysterious, which form a disconcerting whole to the detriment of the simple requirements of sharing, brotherhood and giving and the praxis that goes with these: this has led to a liturgy with no roots in reality and which in most cases leads directly to lack of commitment.

The problem of translation (in the widest sense) thrown up by the situation is certainly a formidable one, but with the progress made by exegesis, semantics and the scientific instruments of hermeneutics there is some justification for thinking that we are better equipped to master them today. We now know the disastrous effect that literal translations, which used to be in favour,[4] can have and we must ask whether it is not better to translate rather more freely, even to transpose in accordance with the context, if we are to translate an author's thought correctly and set it in a different cultural setting. Under the pressure of a general mission situation we must make a radical effort at new translation, which would make the sign more immediately significant of what is signified in the basic essentials.

In order to clarify these ideas I would like to propose a contribution—made from my personalist and active viewpoint—which would provide a new formulation of certain parts of the Our Father, of the account of the institution of the Eucharist and of the Agnus Dei. In each case I will give a quick summary of the pastoral, exegetical or semantic reasoning behind my suggestions, hoping that these efforts by a non-specialist and the research they represent will serve to simulate and provoke specialists to search for the radical renewal of the basic liturgical texts that seems to me both necessary, urgent and perhaps also a stimulus to poets to lend their efforts in this field,[5] as has already been done with a certain measure of success in the new translations of the psalms.

THE LORD'S PRAYER, ITS DOXOLOGY AND EMBOLISM

For the Lord's Prayer, taking the text established in 1966,[6] I will confine myself to three of the final petitions, which I propose to formulate in a more active style:

Instead of saying	I propose
give us this day	help us to produce and share
our daily bread	the bread you give us
forgive us our trespasses	to forgive as you forgive[7].
as we forgive those	and to overcome temptation
who trespass against us	
and lead us not into temptation	

The Doxology and Embolism established at the same time by an ecumenical commission seem to me equally in need of rethinking: 'for the kingdom, the power and the glory are yours' is of course a literal and deliberately archaic use of an old text, but our solutions look forward not backward and I find this doxology at once triumphalist, crushing and vulgar in tone;[8] it is in any case an accumulation of words that are misleading for us; I would rather see a solution on the lines of the following:

for you are the source of joy, of happiness and of peace,
for you are our strength, our life, our peace,
for your kingdom is love where all is forgiven for all to be given
for you offer us a share in your kingdom of love.

Otherwise where in the Lord's Prayer, except indirectly, can one find any suggestion that God is Love and calls us to love in action? And yet this is after all the basic essential of the message and of all mystical life.[9] Whether this is from timidity, clumsiness or simply the expression of a different culture matters little; we are not here to pass judgment on the past, but for our part we have no reason to hide the light under a bushel: therefore we must decode the message for our own time so that its dynamism can direct our action.

THE EUCHARISTIC CELEBRATION

As Jesus bore witness throughout his life, the heart of his message is that we are called to live a life of brotherly love in the dynamic of the Father's love. The eucharistic celebration which lies at the heart of the life of the Church, the memorial of the Lord (a memorial of his whole life as much as of the Last Supper, passion and resurrection) should recapitulate the heart of the message and revive its call to love in us, a call to love in deeds and in truth (1 Jn. 3:18), that is, a call that leads us to action (external action).[10]

I agree of course that the mass is a commitment in charity[11] and its celebration should make this clear. The post-conciliar eucharistic prayers often show a remarkable quality in this respect and express it in a satisfactory way, but it is still true that the centrepiece of the celebration, its kernel, i.e., the *words of institution* as they are said now (and the gestures that accompany them), hardly have any direct bearing on this aspect. Concentration is focused on short and synthetically exceptionally dense propositions, but ones that carry an apparently unwanted symbolism: 'take and eat . . . this is my body, take and drink . . . this is my blood'. One has to accept the fact that for practically all lay people these words have no immediately perceptible meaning and that in themselves they are neither stimulating nor provoking of enthusiasm. Taken literally there is no escape from the fact that they risk being misunderstood and that they generally suggest—even if symbolically—something akin to magic and anthropophagy.[12] There are of course detailed explanations of them in existence but relatively few people have access to these or can remember them alongside the obvious meaning of the words used in order to appreciate their deep significance. Most of the faithful, when they come to the kernel of the celebration, dive straight under blankets of mystery; what actually happens is that each person interprets the words as best he can. Is this really inevitable?

I hardly think so, and besides the aspect of the requirement for order in pastoral matters, there seem to be various exegetical and semantic considerations that would justify (at least in my inexpert opinion) a new non-literal translation and even a fair degree of freedom in transposition. I would like to put forward the following reasons for this:

(a) We know today that these words are not the *ipsissima verba* of Jesus but a synthetic and symbolic literary composition designed for liturgical use in a particular cultural milieu (The exact words after all differ somewhat with different authors and traditions);

(b) We also know that the words, *bread, flesh, life* and *blood* all have connotations in the Semitic languages that no literal translation can capture (the same goes for the choice of the species[13]);

(c) We know today that non-verbal expression is at least as meaningful as spoken words and that it enables us to interpret words.[14]

Let us look a little closer at this last point: in their accounts of the Last Supper the Synoptics and I Cor. all pick out the gesture of sharing the bread and the gesture of sharing the wine; the Acts speak of the breaking of bread (in order to share it round). It was in this gesture of Jesus—in which he put his whole self because it summed up his whole life, in which everything was shared—a life totally given (even to dying for those he loved)—that his disciples were to recognise him after his resurrection; it was this gesture that summed up his last commandments to the disciples—the *mandatum;* it was through this gesture that they would celebrate him and steep themselves in his thought and his ethics.[15]

(d) The overall context of the Gospels should therefore shed light on these words and their immediate context should allow us to reconstruct them if they were lost. Conversely, detached from the Gospel, these words would have neither meaning nor interest. The commandment that went with these gestures: 'Do this in memory of me', which John places after the service of washing the feet (another significant gesture), could well refer not only to a repetition of these gestures at the Last Supper, but to the call to live in this way as he had done throughout his life, which he was then symbolically summing up: the deeds of true love. The celebration then becomes a link between past experience and future experience in union with Jesus and with what he lived and preached, or again a reminder, a stimulus, the renewal of our hopes and of our determination to act: this is why it is a feast.

If we go back to the words traditionally used it should be possible to sketch out a more flexible variation: on the one hand the *flesh and blood* mean the whole person in his historical embodiment, as is well known,[16] and not certain component parts taken separately; on the other hand these words form a commentary on a gesture of sharing; one could therefore translate the sharing of the bread by: 'This is me', in which the word *this* would designate the gesture of sharing; it would then mean a symbolism in action and one that leads to action.[17] As for the sharing of the cup, this is a gesture of fraternization leading those who take part in it into a sort of consanguinity (through alliance), which is a very different gesture, not a simple repetition of the preceding one—from which it is in any case separated by the length of a meal[18]— and one translated better by the versions given by Luke and Paul than by those of Matthew and Mark: 'this cup is the new alliance in my blood'; such an interpretation could justify a less frequent usage than the breaking of the bread.

Another little-used element of flexibility lies in the fact that, as we know, the verb *to be* in the Semitic languages cannot figure in these propositions. Pastor Westphal has not hesitated to translate them; 'this *represents* my body. . . . this *symbolizes* the alliance in my blood' (*Encyclopaedic Dictionary of the Bible,* 1956).

Once what is meant has been clearly perceived, one should be able to express it, without separating it from the event-institution, through new gestures and new words (and new species), which would express it in the most meaningful way possible. So it would seem desirable for specialists to follow this line further than I can, perhaps bearing in mind that such a transposition could be justified by taking the idea of *transfinalization* put forward more than ten years ago by Schillebeeckx.

It would surely be in accordance with the directives of the Conciliar Constitution on the Liturgy[19] to express the essence of the institution in simple gestures and words whose meaning and significance would immediately be clear to anyone belonging to the culture for which they were composed. It would also have an entirely beneficial effect in countries where mission and catechesis operate under restraint and even clandestinely. Finally it would open up a wide field of agreement in the ecumenical dialogue.[20]

By way of illustrating these suggestions, here are two attempts to reformulate the account of institution using free transposition, in which the commitment of those who take part is embodied, so that proclamation of the Word and of orthodox belief call immediately for orthopraxis:

We celebrate Jesus Christ
who was love personified,
to make us love one another even more.
He brings us together
in the sign of the bread and wine we share
as he did with his friends
the day before his passion and his last supper.
He put his whole life and message into this gesture

and his disciples always recognized him by it.[21]
That evening, as he shared the bread and wine,
he gave thanks to his Father
and said: Here is my life and my blood,
given from love for you and for all,
to set you free and unite you in love.
Go and do the same:
Love one another as I have loved you,
and in me you will have life and joy without end.

We have come together to remember Jesus,
to live his life and to carry it on.
Having loved his people,
he loved them to the end.
At his last meal,
as he was giving his life for his friends,
he shared the bread and wine and said:
I have given everything:
Go and do the same.
Eat my bread, drink my wine and live my life
and you will have life and joy to the full.
Now we who share this bread and this wine,
who come together in the body of Christ to be one body
and become brothers in the alliance of his blood to be one blood,
pledge ourselves to live
a life of service to our brothers
like him and in union with him,
to build a more just and brotherly world
and so possess the fulness of his life and his joy.

THE AGNUS DEI

'Lamb of God . . . have mercy on us . . . give us your peace'.

In so far as this ancient text responds well to certain aspects of our human condition, particularly to certain extreme conditions,[22] and is well-suited to a sorrowing and passive type of spirituality, so it can be challenged virtually in its entirety by other aspects of the economy of salvation and in particular by a personalist spirituality.

According to Baumstark, the liturgical usage of this invocation goes back to the eighth century; it has often been justified by reference to one of the passages describing the *suffering Servant* of Isaiah. 'he opened not his mouth, like a *lamb* led to the slaughter' (Is. 53:7). This is usually left at that, and argued for a particular type of theology of suffering and the Cross and a passive route to salvation:[23] one suffers evil, one is delivered from it by the intervention of God alone; one can but suffer, pray, beseech and wait for it to pass; one is reduced to an objective and passive mode of behaviour, however valid and conscious this may be. This is a logical interpretation in one sense and yet many find it suspect and even intolerable; we should therefore see if there is not another equally possible interpretation.

In fact there is a whole other school of theology that appeals to our co-operation in God's work. Following St Paul (1 Cor. 3:9), St Augustine was already thinking in this way when he wrote: 'God who created you without your help does not save you without your help'. And there is one of the Beatitudes that refers to the *peacemakers* and the active role expected of them. Another refers to those who struggle and who suffer persecution for justice's sake. More recently, in the school of the theology of liberation, Dom Fragoso has written: 'When the Gospel is preached in such a way that it moves us to passivity, resignation, conformism and acceptance of every injustice, it is no longer the Gospel of Jesus Christ'.[24] Now there is no doubt that our *Agnus Dei* runs the risk of inducing this sort of behaviour.

It is quite possible to reinterpret the prophetic witness of Isaiah in this other sense without having to reject it. One only has to read the same passage to the end and take account of what follows. Isaiah in fact says of the suffering servant: 'he offers his life . . . he gave himself up' (which has been taken up in the fourth eucharistic prayer, following Jn. 10:11, 15, 18). This is the very antithesis of what is suggested by the passive, suffering and naive image of the lamb: here we have a deliberate choice, the courageous voluntary act that belongs rather to the image of the *hero* (Is. 49:2, 24).[25]

Furthermore, modern exegesis and semantics have opened up other possibilities. For Dodd, rather than a lamb, the image is one of a ram or a scapegoat, a leader in the battle; it is in any case not the same image as the paschal lamb (except by a vague analogy). According to Ball, there is probably a play on words (or even a confusion) between *Taleh* which in Hebrew means 'lamb', and *Talya* which means 'servant' in Aramaic.

We are then at least in a position to say: 'Servant of God, you take on the sin of the world. . . .'

The image of the lamb is not only somewhat devoid of interest but can lend itself to considerable confusion, particularly with children who are liable to forget what animal they are supposed to be dealing with. One suggestion, made by Patrice de la Tour du Pin, was that to avoid the passivity and *naiveté* associated with the image of a lamb (let alone that of a sheep), the term should be replaced in a freely composed eucharistic prayer with the image of a *horse,* whose courage, intelligence and loyalty are proverbial. However, whatever animal is chosen, one can perhaps question whether any zoological symbolism—abundantly used in the Bible and belonging to that sort of agropastoral civilization—still has sufficient power of evocation in our predominantly technical and urban civilization. Apart from this, the conscious and clear choice of a man risking his life can hardly be compared to an animal whatever its merits.

So I would prefer once again to abandon the imagery and go for clarity of meaning: what we are trying to say is that he gave his life for us and calls on us to do the same (and not just to lament while thinking of the 'sacrificed victim' and saying 'Lord, Lord'). If we take this line, we would have something like the following:

> Lord Jesus,
> you give your life
> for love of us.
> Make us share better,
> make us give ourselves better,
> make us build peace,
> make us find your joy.

BY WAY OF CONCLUSION

From the time of preparation for the second Vatican Council, and particularly since the Council, much has been done to bring our liturgy up to date. One cannot but be glad of this, but if we are to express our faith and its celebration for our time in terms compatible with an active and committed life today, there is still much to do, and I have no doubt that in this field, as in others, we are on the way to 'renewing the face of the earth' with the help of the Holy Spirit. But if we are to give the Church back a new youth, we have to show as much imagination, courage and audacity in the face of our persecutors as the first Christians did. Perhaps these suggestions can help a little on the way so that we can then go straight from celebrating to practising our eucharist.

Translated by Ian Buons

Notes

1. In Catholic Action we tend to talk about the need for *witness*, but this, unlike charity, is not an end in itself; it is only a result of experience, but its

setback should worry us and make us question the quality of our experience. Cf. P. Régamey, 'Charité d'abord: qu'est-ce à dire?', in *Cahiers St Jacques* (1974).

2. 'We shall be judged on love', said St John of the Cross: this does not imply a hesitant morality but a dynamic of love (*virtus*): that 'harlots can precede us into the Kingdom of Heaven' should make us think.

3. Which is the justification of 'charismatics' against the hierarchy. . . .

4. 'Literal translation produces errors of interpretation. . . . One must translate and even transpose': M. Riquet, 'Une traduction nécessaire', in *Foi et Langage*, 1 (1976).

5. We are not short of either exegetes or poets, but they have too often been rejected, alienated, discouraged and muzzled.

6. The (French) text adopted (cf. *La Maison Dieu*, 85 [1966]) was severely criticized by J. Carmignac, *Recherches sur le Notre Père* (Paris, 1969).

7. Cf. Lk. 6: 36-8.

8. There was an enquiry before it was adopted. I was one of those who challenged and objected to the formula proposed.

9. The same applies to the traditional *Credos,* but equivalent hymns and chants take account of this need today.

10. The external act remains the touchstone: cf Jn. 4:20, etc.

11. This was the theme of a seminar held in France in 1950 by C.P.L. (*Centre de Pastorale Liturgique*): cf. *La Maison Dieu* 24 (1950).

12. In this respect, it seems to me unfortunate that the post-conciliar eucharistic prayers should have kept the expression, 'the bread and wine that will *become* the body and blood of Christ', which is more likely to lead to error than talk of a new 'meaning'. Catechists now talk of the 'mysterious transformation' of the bread and wine into the body and blood of Christ—the sacrament is turned into magic. H. Haddad entitled his account of the Andes survival through cannibalism *La Cène* (*The Supper*). (P. P. Read's English title *Alive:* avoided this unfortunate interpretation, which was nevertheless felt by the survivors themselves . . . *Trans.*)

13. On the symbolic level, the object is designed to have a function of meaningful communication: it should also be capable of being *translated;* the event commemorated has to be *actualized,* which excludes an imitative reproduction. See my article, 'La dernière Cène et l'institution eucharistique', in *Notre Combat* (Apr. 1976). In some parts, the bread and wine could well be replaced by rice or millet and beer or tea.

14. Cf. H. Schurmann, 'The words of Jesus at the Last Supper in the Light of his Actions', in *Concilium* 40 (1968); F. Leehman, *La Parole visible* (Paris, 1971).

15. Cf. Lk. 24: 35; Jn. 15: 12; Acts 3: 42, etc.

16. Cf. the Jerusalem Bible commentary on Jn. 1:14 and Mt. 16: 15.

17. Several writers (Jeremias, Kilmartin, Mertens) envisage such an interpretation; many of the Old Testament prophets, in order to make their points (and from their Semitic mode of expression) joined a symbolic gesture to their words, to make a symbolic action, or described the gesture itself. Did Diogenes not demonstrate movement by walking? There is a Spanish proverb that says:

'*Lo que se oye, se escucha; lo que se ve, se imita*' (You listen to what you hear; you copy what you see). Furthermore, an exemplary gesture both evokes and provokes orthopraxis, while the *thing* itself (with words) produces contemplation and orthodox commentaries. By saying: 'He put his whole life and message into this gesture', I mean in the first place that at the Last Supper (or after the Resurrection) this gesture added something to his physical presence; later, in our celebration of the event, his *presence* is signified, in a dynamic way, by this *gesture of sharing* rather than by the material nature of the (statically) *transfinalized* species.

18. The French expression 'boire un coup' (originally 'boire une coupe') implies the notion of drinking together, of 'fraternizing'; rather like the 'loving cup' of some traditional occasions, or the 'pipe of peace' of the American Indians; they are eminently collective gestures that express a *community of hope*.

19. 'There will be no need of lengthy explanations for it to be understood' (*Const. on the Liturgy*, n. 34).

20. God incarnate = love personified (in our midst).

21. This gesture, repeated in memory of him, in union with him, becomes a symbolic manifestation of his presence.

22. There are moments when man can do nothing except call on God for mercy: moments of personal tragedy, of natural disaster, times of sickness or of consciousness of the 'tragic sense of life'. Suffering can be transfigured through God's help, but it is still an evil that we must fight by the means at our command, and the worst evils are those caused by man (actively or passively): cf. M. Zundel, *Quel homme, quel Dieu* (Paris, 1976), p. 103. Hence the capital importance of evoking the part that depends on us.

23. The old theme of Christian resignation, exaggerated into 'Dolourism' and a certain sort of theology of the Cross, challenged by theologians for the past fifty years, attacked by Mounier, still lingers on in liturgical language. It will be difficult to root it out, but it must be done: cf. D. Duquoc, 'The Cross of Christ and Human Suffering', in *Concilium* 119 (1976).

24. Dom Fragoso, *Evangile et révolution sociale* (Paris, 1969).

25. At the Congress of the World Union of Christian Democrats held in Rome in December 1975, Paul VI declared: The name of Christian can be a sign of contradiction and even call for *heroism*' (i.e., there is no more talk of passive suffering).

Jean-Claude Sagne

Literature on Charisms and the Charismatic Movements: Inner Healing

OF the many publications which are now showing a rapid increase in charismatic circles I have severely limited my choice to those dealing with 'inner healing'.

Inner healing is the overflowing of a spiritual experience into our affectivity, inducing peace and joy, reconciliation and unity. The topic may well appear too restricted. Its importance lies in that it demands an elaboration of spiritual experience as a whole. To speak of inner healing amounts to surveying the ways of the spiritual life and the encounter with God. Moreover, the subject is not only of theoretical interest. From a particular angle inner healing reveals that purifying process of the spiritual experience which authenticates it and makes it last.

On this subject of inner healing I have made use of three books. They form the basis for the reflections which I shall put forward. The first is by Michael Scanlan: *Inner Healing* (New York, Paulist Press, 1974). The second is by Francis MacNutt, O.P.: *Healing* (Notre Dame, Indiana, Ave Maria Press, 1974). The third by Ovila Melançon, C.S.C.: *Guérison et Renouveau charismatique* (Healing and charismatic renewal, Canada, 1976). All three are Catholic priests belonging to the Movement for Charismatic Renewal.

By dealing in my own way with the spiritual experience which these authors describe I have no intention whatever of opposing negative criticisms to this or that point of their teaching. The lived experience which is the source of their inspiration is also what I live by. Having belonged to the charismatic renewal since 1973 I simply wish to set out clearly and comprehensibly a point of wisdom about what we have been given to live by where inner healing is concerned. I will arrange my thoughts around three themes: the spiritual context of inner healing, the ways in which inner healing proceeds, and the lessons to be drawn from inner healing.

THE SPIRITUAL CONTEXT OF INNER HEALING

Inner healing is different from both physical and spiritual healing (cf. MacNutt, *op. cit.*, p. 163). Physical healing takes place when an organic illness disappears and one sees there God's intervention. God's healing deed may go through many channels, and, to start with, through treatment by doctors and the effect of prescribed medicine. The essence of physical healing is that it is seen as a gift of God himself. Spiritual healing is God's forgiveness which enables us to be repentant, to renounce our sin and to leave ourselves open to a new life ruled by charity.

Inner healing is far more subtle and difficult to describe and define, for all depends on what is meant here by 'inner'. I begin with Michael Scanlan's definition: 'Inner healing is the healing of the inner man. By "inner man" we mean the spheres of the intellect, the emotions and the will, generally called reason, heart and will'. Inner healing therefore is a healing of the psyche. It does not immediately concern the relation to God and the God-oriented life but the organization of our intelligence, our will, our memory and our emotional sensitivity. In the broad sense one might say that inner healing is the healing of the heart in so far as the heart is the place where the life of grace and our emotional sensitivity meet.

Explaining inner healing is in no way an explanation of the development of a person-to-person relationship and still less an inventory of recipes or adaptation techniques. Inner healing begins with gazing upon Jesus who, through the power and sweetness of the Spirit, brought complete healing to multitudes of sick people. Now 'Jesus Christ is the same yesterday and today and for ever' (Hebrews, 13:8). Inner healing refers first of all to the power of healing which Jesus exercises today in his Church in those who ask him with faith. Thus inner healing is an act of Jesus himself in the heart of the faithful. Though it must not be confused with spiritual healing it cannot be separated from it because it even seems to be a consequence and extension of it.

Recourse to inner healing supposes a truly spiritual concept of psychical troubles, and even mental illness. Faced with any lasting difficulty which we experience in the functioning of our psyche, whether it con-

cerns our judgment or our emotional state, we should examine ourselves in order to bring to light a possibly spiritual root of our trouble.
Not every psychical difficulty is the consequence of a sin. The way in
which we experience the difficulty today in our life may give us some
indication about its origin. When a health affliction is accepted in peace
and praise, there is no particular reason to look for its origin in some
previous offence. But when psychical troubles are mixed up with difficulties in believing, praying, trusting the Lord, the question about the
spiritual origin of it all arises. Sin in our past always leaves traces in the
sense that it makes it more difficult for us to accept and master ourselves. Both original and personal sin is the root cause of all human
misery (Melançon, *op. cit.*).

One of the most characteristic consequences of personal sin is that it
creates one or more spiritual ties. This fact, very difficult to recapture,
needs some explanation. When we let ourselves be guided by the image
of a 'tie' we see that the tie is a kind of bond which more or less
profoundly hampers our spiritual freedom and, because of that, prevents us from abandoning ourselves totally to the love of God. One can
recognize the existence of such spiritual ties by a number of indications. One's mood is unstable, and there are sudden fits of sadness,
anger or depression. The believer often finds it difficult to pray, to read
the Word of God, to receive the sacraments (especially that of reconciliation), to abandon oneself to God like a child, to put one's trust in
the Virgin Mary. When there is a spiritual tie the peace of faith is often
impaired and the prayer of praise is almost impossible.

This tie is the trace of previous sins which have allowed our trust in
God to be cut into. At the heart of most of those ties there is fear, fear
of the past or the future, fear of falling or relapsing, fear of losing those
dear to us or goods which give us an illusory sense of security. They
often spring from occult practices or from contamination by eastern
religions.

At the origin of these spiritual ties there is often a reconciliation
which has not been granted or a pardon of God which has not been
accepted: 'No sin blocks the power of God's healing so seriously as the
refusal of forgiveness' (Melançon, *op. cit.*).

The spiritualties which render a soul captive make us look again at
healing in the New Testament where Jesus usually links the prayer for
delivery with the request for healing. The tie shows the power of him
who renders us captive by making the fear of death weigh us down,
Satan in person (cf. Heb. 2:14–5). The model of healing is provided by
Jesus when he healed a woman who was sick as a result of diabolical
possession: 'And ought not this woman, a daughter of Abraham whom
Satan bound for eighteen years, be loosed from this bond on the sab-
bath day?' (Lk. 13:16).

The discovery of these spiritual ties, their nature and the degree of their seriousness takes place in prayer where the Spirit endows the brethren with the necessary discernment. It is not the object of a self-knowledge worked out all by oneself.

METHODS OF INNER HEALING

The deliverance from spiritual ties by the power of the Spirit is not usually an end in itself, but rather a starting-point. This deliverance is like going through a gateway which puts one on the way towards inner healing. Here again the image of the tie is evocative. When someone has been carrying a chain for some time, he suffers the painful marks and paralyzing after-effects of it, even after the chain has been taken off. There is a time for all things, and so there is a time for re-learning how to walk upright and in freedom. Most often this inner healing is a long process because it develops in us according to the rhythm of the growth of our belief in God and our abandoning ourselves to his fatherly love.

Inner healing starts with a prayer of request, formulated by the sufferer, supported as far as possible by the prayer of several brethren. What is noteworthy is that inner healing often requires perseverance in prayer on both sides (cf. MacNutt, *op. cit.*, p. 182; Melançon, *op. cit.*).

The very fact of this perseverance in prayer is practising that fidelity to the faith which is the main source of inner healing. God only asks to give. Jesus surely wants to deliver the faithful from what prevents them from abandoning themselves to the stirring and inspiration of the Spirit. For that reason, the efficacy of the prayer for healing, based on the assured gift of God, depends on the quality of the faith of him for whom one prays and of all those who pray with and for him (cf. Melançon, *op. cit.*).

Trust in God's gift of inner healing is normally expressed by continuous prayer in simplicity of heart and by assiduous reading of the Word of God. More than in any other kind of prayer, it is in the prayer of praise that healing is received, because praise purifies us by making us no longer see ourselves as the centre in order to turn to the God of mercy and by assimilating us to him through our constantly renewed gazing upon him. At the heart as at the end of praise it is still more particularly the prayer of adoration which opens us up to the God who is coming and builds us up again. Located within the whole of the life of faith, inner healing flows through the action of the sacraments, particularly those of reconciliation and the Eucharist (cf. MacNutt, *op. cit.*, p. 184). Inner healing cannot be dissociated from all the labour of purification and sanctification which God's grace works in us.

As it proceeds patiently and perseveringly in the faith, inner healing is granted by God as we pass through events and encounters, in a way that is very simple and ordinary. Through prayer, memories of emotional hurts from early childhood or more recent times gently come back to us. Dreams, symbolic behaviour or inner visions bring about a kind of remodelling of the personality or of the broken heart. The Spirit's way of teaching is very simple and very personal. He gives each what suits him, at the opportune time and in the right way. What is most important is that those who pray for inner healing do not yield to any temptation of impatience or lack of delicacy but in true love await God's time, at the same time respecting most carefully the freedom of their suffering brethren (Scanlan, *op. cit.*).

LESSONS TO BE DRAWN FROM INNER HEALING

The experience of prayer for inner healing teaches us a great deal about spiritual experience, which, for a large part, it overlaps with. It shows that the essence of spiritual experience is not the explicit exercise of this or that charism but rather the manifestation of the fruits of the Spirit, which arise from charity, and are: 'love, joy, peace, patience, kindness, goodness, faithfulness, gentleness, self-control . . .' (Gal. 5:22–3).

Inner healing reveals the depth of man's inner life which really only emerges in persevering and contemplative prayer. Faith is an abyss. Between the soul, root of our being, source of our life, in which God, Creator and Saviour, is present, on the one hand, and our emotional life woven together by imaginings and analyzable feelings on the other, *the heart is located*. This is not just an image or a kind of comparison. The heart is definitely a locus of human sensibility which the Spirit sets free and brings to life. Thus inner healing brings to life or revives in us feelings of praise, joy, compassion or compunction which are truly our human feelings but only come to light through the effect of liberating and healing grace. This new heart, set free from the depth of our self by the Spirit, is the centre of our human experience of God in so far as it ensures communication between the gifts of God and our lived human reality where we sense it in our whole emotional personality and in all our behaviour.

At a still deeper level, inner healing invites us to meditate on the active and passive purification of our life of faith under the influence of the Spirit (cf. Melançon, *op. cit.*). This point seems extremely important to me for a progress in faith and prayer which is a continuing process and seeks to be confirmed in the truth. To sum up I would say that the active purification of the faith tends to make us live the faith in all its purity, supported only by the Word of God. Nothing purifies so much as the practice of pure faith. As to passive purification, this aims principally at making us realize our weakness through trials, temptation, the solitude of the heart and inner silence. The deepest passive purification is therefore the knowledge which God himself gives us of our sin. The humility which results from it opens our heart to the gift of God. This is why the whole process of inner healing takes place in the presence of the Virgin Mary whose whole mystery consists of faith, humility and purity. By teaching us to be very small Mary makes us grow in the faith which exposes us unreservedly to the action of the Spirit who purifies us, heals us, and renews us.

Contributors

PAUL ABELA was born in Cairo in 1921, and has lived in Paris since 1950. He is a married civil engineer and has been interested actively in third-world problems, and biblical and liturgical renewal, based on personalist inspiration. He is a member of the French Socialist Party and he has published articles and reviews in spiritual and theological journals.

LADISLAUS BOROS is an established theologian. He was born in Budapest in 1927 and has studied theology and philosophy in many European countries. He is Honorary Professor of the Philosophy of Religion at Innsbruck University and lives as an independent writer in Switzerland. Among his many influential works are *The Mystery of Death, Meeting God in Man* and *We Are Future*.

CHRISTIAN DUQUOC, O.P., was ordained priest in 1953. He teaches dogmatic theology at the Theological Faculty of Lyon University and is a member of the Editorial Board of the journal *Lumière et Vie*. Among his major works are the two volumes of a *Christologie* (Paris, 1972).

ENRIQUE DUSSEL was born in Mendoz, Argentina, in 1934. He is a Professor in the Faculty of Philosophy and Humanities of the Independent University of Mexico and of the Department of Religious Sciences of the Ibero-American University (Mexico). He is the author of several major works on anthropology, Latin-American history, liberation, and the Hispano-American hierarchies.

CLAUDE GEREST, O.P., was born at Saint-Etienne, France, in 1921. He teaches at the Lyon and Viviers seminaries, lectures in the Catholic Faculties of Lyon, is attached to the St Irenée ecumenical centre, and writes for *Lumière et Vie*.

RENE LAURENTIN was born at Tours, France, in 1917 and is Professor of Theology at the Catholic University of Angers. He has taught at several foreign universities, is religious correspondent for the French daily newspaper *Le Figaro* and is the author of several major works on theology and spirituality, notably a recent study of Pentecostalism.

JEAN-CLAUDE SAGNE, O.P., was born at Tours in 1936 and was ordained a priest in 1963. He teaches psychology in the Catholic Faculties in Lyon and at the University of Lyon II. Among his publications are studies of sin, guilt, penitence and conversion.

LUIGI SARTORI was born in 1924 in Roana, Vicenza, Italy and was ordained priest in 1946. He is Professor of Theology at the episcopal seminary of Padua and in the Theological Faculty of Milan University. He is President of the Italian Theological Association. Among his books are studies of Blondel and of the theology of history.

RAUL VIDALES was born in 1943 in Monterrey, Mexico. He has taught sociology and theology in various Latin-American universities. He is now at the Bartolomé de las Casas Centre at Lima, Peru and at the CENAMI, Mexico. Among his publications are studies of the Church and politics since Medellín and of the theology of liberation.